The Life of One Called and Chosen

Elzora McEwen Golden

with Barbara Hollace

I0175028

Published by Hollace House Publishing Spokane Valley, Washington
The Life of One Called and Chosen: Elzora McEwen Golden

Copyright © 2025 Elzora Golden
All rights reserved.

No part of this publication may be reproduced, stored in a retrieval system, or
transmitted in any form by any means, electronic, mechanical, photocopying,
recording, or by any information retrieval or storage system without the
express written permission of the author except in the case of excerpts used
for critical review.

Scripture taken from the New King James Version®. Copyright © 1982 by Thomas Nelson. Used by
permission. All rights reserved. All other verses quoted are King James Version, public domain.

Book editing: Barbara Hollace, www.barbarahollace.com
Book layout/cover design: Russ Davis, Bravo Book Design, www.bravobookdesign.com
Photography: Golden family photos

ISBN: 979-8-9927741-7-7

Printed in the United States of America

Dedication

This book is dedicated to my Father, God.
Loving Husband, Paul
And our children and their children
Dan & Karen, Mason, Madison & Danielle
Lelia & Wayne, Jeremy, Amber, Harmony & grandchildren
Diana, Sarah, Jessica & grandchildren
Tim & Cheryl, Lance

Contents

Introduction

To everything there is a season, a time for every purpose under heaven.
~ Ecclesiastes 3:1

Every book is an adventure because every life is an adventure. God wrote a book about our lives before we were born (Psalm 139:16).

I heard your story is a bestseller in heaven!

In 2008, when my husband and I moved to Spokane Valley, Washington, we met a couple at church. They soon "adopted" us and would give us a ride to church since we had no car. They called us "kids" which made my husband chuckle.

We quickly learned that Zoe was quite a prayer warrior. Together with her husband Paul, they were greatly loved at the church, Spokane Dream Center. They held a special place in our hearts, too.

Since I am an author myself and book editor, it doesn't take long for the conversation to turn toward the book a person has always been intending to write. It came up in my conversation with Zoe as well.

So over the years, there has been the talk about a book about her life… or maybe more than one book. Zoe has had a very "interesting" life as she describes it. Most of us would say it rises higher than the level of interesting.

Zoe is an amazing woman of God who has said yes to many God adventures. Now in her early nineties, some health issues have been nipping at her heels. The urgency to get the book finished has accelerated over the last year, and especially in recent months.

A little over a year ago, after both Paul and Zoe encountered some severe health issues, they moved to be with their family, a little over two hours away. Not exactly the five minute stop off at their place that it used to be.

So Zoe and I have been collaborating on this book long distance. A special thanks to George and Margaret Lopez for the many trips to visit Zoe and Paul to continue putting this book together.

It's more than a book. It's the legacy of a mighty prayer warrior who has much to teach us about spiritual warfare and walking close with the Lord. Zoe's never give up attitude and great faith has brought her this far. And her lessons have brought many of us to a higher level in our Christian walk as well.

As with any book, you can't capture every piece of a person's journey. Those of you who have met Zoe in person or had a phone conversation with her will be blessed by the laughter you hear between the lines and her strong voice as she commands the enemy to flee, in Jesus' name.

With a long journey, there are often casualties along the way. In this case, one of them is a missing volume of stories. It's disappeared and has never been located. So, if you are reading this book and you happen to be the one who Zoe entrusted with this sacred treasure, please contact me. We could do a second edition of this book with more adventures!

God only knows the number of Zoe's days. But what I know is this, I am blessed to call her friend, prayer warrior, mentor. She has been my Elijah during the last eighteen years of my life. Her lessons will live on beyond her and the seeds she has sown into me, have been sown into the lives of others.

Zoe Golden, thank you for loving God and for loving us. Well done, good and faithful servant!

—Barbara Hollace

Just a Glimpse...

(Note: This list was created some years ago, so numbers may have changed.)
Throughout the years, I've been to:
Heaven, eight times (at least 20 times, currently).
Russia, one time
China, one time
Mexico, three times
Africa, three times
Spain, one time

First time in heaven

When I was 17, I was in an accident and I was taken by Jesus to heaven and hell. Jesus let me know I was dying, and had not repented, and did not know the Lord. Jesus gave me a chance to accept Him in a coma. I did and God healed me through Jesus Christ, our Lord.

Second time in heaven (Phoenix, Arizona)

I was sick for three days. Each day I went to heaven. The first day I saw my father and we visited all day. He would introduce me to people as they went by. My father would say I was there visiting. The second day I knew a lot of people there and they confirmed some revelations God had been giving me.

The third day I met Alberta's mother in heaven. I only knew her from the picture I had of hers. She was 93 years old in the picture. But when I saw her in heaven, she was the age of 25. She had on a royal blue dress with white flowers. She came across the lawn and talked to me in (thoughts). We did not need to talk out loud.

As we talked, she came into the room where I was sick and said, "Father, heal this child." I woke up out of my sickness and saw her walk through the walls in a blue mist and back to heaven.

I got out of bed as though I had never been sick. I went into the living room and sat in the rocking chair that had once been hers. She came and laid her hand on my shoulder and said, "Are you alright, daughter?" I said, "Yes." And she was gone.

Fifth time in heaven

I was caught up into heaven at night. When I arrived at my mother's place, I asked her for one of her gowns to put on as I was in my nightgown. She gave me one and it was glowing with

God's glory on it. We visited all night. I also saw some men going by with glorified clothes on. It was wonderful there. My mother had a big veranda to her house and that's where we visited.

Sixth time in heaven

I was caught up into a beautiful place and the country was beautiful. Abraham came and put his hand on my shoulder and said it all belongs to you. Zoe, go in and possess it.

Seventh time in heaven

When I was in Bible school, we drove up on a hillside overlooking the valley and I was caught up into a vision of heaven. I saw the trees with all manner of fruit on them, also leaves for the healing of the nations.

Eighth time in heaven

Recently I was caught up into heaven for two seconds, I saw my mother and waved at her. Her hair was almost black. She looked young and I waved at her. Also I saw Bill Purfoy who is now in heaven almost two years. Two seconds up, two seconds back.

August 28, 2018

Bill Purfoy came and waved a blue and black flag or maybe it was a blue and black cloth. Anyways he told me God was pleased. I had asked to have him send me help to do my book. This is what he said, "Out of the blue, God would send me someone to help me and the black was the ink to write it."

The Story Begins

The Story Begins...

This story begins January 11, 1932. A little girl by the name of Elzora Jane (nickname Zoe) was born to Gladys and Lee McEwen.

My oldest brother Kenny told me a doctor flew out to the homestead to deliver me. This was near Los Alamos, Colorado. While on this homestead, I remember my brother Melvin turning on the windmill and pumping water into a big round water tank basin. Then on the hot days, my brothers and sisters would swim in it. Of course it was for the horses and cows to drink out of. I was three years old at the time and enjoying watching them have fun.

* * *

When I was three years old I remember living in Oklahoma, where Dad was raising goats. Dad had bought a new car with a canvas top. The two goats got up on top of the car and put their feet through the roof. Dad became angry and killed the two goats. Dinner was had out of them for days to come. Dad sold the rest of the goats. There were no more car problems.

You will hear more of the Drylands (homestead) by my brother Kenny as he wrote down some things for me, as I was too little to remember it all.

* * *

Because of the Dust Bowl, my folks moved to Oklahoma. Then they had some friends living in Castle Rock, Washington who encouraged them to move to Washington state. Told them money grew on trees and bushes. Of course they were speaking of blackberries, Cassava bark on trees, ferns in the woods. Strawberries on bushes. Blackberries, raspberries.

So the folks moved to Washington state in 1936 and settled in Toledo, Washington. We lived on what was called the river bottom. We drove down a steep hill and at the bottom was a spring of water where people came from all over to get the water to drink and take home with them in barrels.

My sister lived on a ranch that had gas in the water near Spirit Lake. They hauled barrels of this water for their cooking and bathing, etc.

We lived on the river bottom for many years. During this time, we planted gardens, harvested fruit off old homesteads. Mom dried apples which we ate in the winter. Canned vegetables, beef, salmon, deer, and pork. She always had food to give away. She prayed a lot while on the river bottom. We had good neighbors. One lady in particular. She took care of us when Dad and Mom went to Portland to work in the shipyard. We all called her Grandma Wales.

She would tell us Bible stories and read to us daily out of God's Word. Because of her, I'm sure I became a Christian later. I believe all nine of us know the Lord.

Some neighbors had a Ouija board. It turns some evil spirits loose in her house. They called Mom to come help them pray it out. They got rid of the board. I was young and quite impressed.

* * *

We finally moved from the river bottom to a place my Uncle Ted owned called the Tate place. Dad rented it until he could build a house on 40 acres he bought called the home place. Just two miles from Toledo, Washington. We had cows and would ride on their tails until we got to the bottom of the hill. If Dad had caught us, I'm sure we would've got a spanking. (Oh, such fun we had there.)

* * *

My father worked for Weyerhaeuser as a timber faller. He made good money but we were always poor. We lived in the new house he built out of used lumber. We had an outdoor toilet and no running water in the house. We had to heat the water for baths on a wood stove, also to wash dishes. These were the Depression years. Dad was an alcoholic and a womanizer. It was such a sad way to live. There were nine of us, though many of us left home early in life.

We had milk and sold milk to a dairy farm where they had it processed. Mom made homemade bread and would fry it and put sugar on it. Nice to eat after school when we came home.

We had chickens who produced eggs for us, also fried them. Yummy, yummy! Dad raised pigs for meat. Also beef cattle for meat. Deer meat was accessible. Salmon was caught in the river with the game warden's permission as we were a large family.

Dad killed a bear one time but it's meat was very bad tasting. So much for bear meat.

* * *

During the years on the home place, we would climb trees, ride horses with our friend who came out from the city. There was a bull that would chase us up a tree and Mom or a neighbor would come get us down. They ended up killing the bull as he was mean. He cornered Mom in this feeding house once, I'm sure it scared her.

My brother Marvin, just older than I, was up on the top of the chicken house trying to call my mother. She'd gone to bring the cows in and it was getting dark. As he would start to call Mom, a chicken would make a terrible sound, he could not hear if she answered. He took out his slingshot and hit the chicken on its head. It went around in a circle and then down to the ground. He thought he had killed it. He got down, ran and got some water, and put it on its head. It came to life ran in the circle and left. We were glad as Dad would've disciplined him. So much for living in the country.

*   *   *

It was never an easy life with dad. He drank all the time and fought with Mr. Cooper, a neighbor man. We fought with the neighbor kids just because Dad did. Later in life, we were very close friends. (All of his kids).

My dad was mean to my mom. When he came home drunk, we would crawl under the table until he went to bed.

My older brother took up wrestling so he could take care of Dad. When Dad started on mother one night, my brother upset Dad, twisted his arm, saying, "You hurt, Mom, again and I'll take care of you." Dad behaved himself after that. (Dad was 6 feet tall. My brother was 5'6" tall.)

*   *   *

My father bought a horse at the sale barn and did not know it was a racehorse. My brothers and I came home from school and found him in the corral. As young folks will do, my brother said I could not sound like a horse, so I let out with a whinny. All of a sudden, the horse jumped the fence and stood under the window where I was sounding off. (Surprise!) We had fun getting him back in the corral.

Dad hooked up the horse to a cultivator so he could get the place ready for the garden. He took off with the horse pulling him out onto the tongue of the cultivator. It was going up and down. Dad was hanging on for dear life. We kids sure enjoyed it as it was so funny. Remember, he was a racehorse. Dad sold him but not before all of us kids had a good time riding him.

My brother Marvin would whistle and get him to go with us on it, then he would take us out in the pasture and he would stop. We could not whistle. So we had to get off and walk home. (No fun.)

We were allowed to ride a neighbor's horse and my brother Marvin was showing off to his friends like a Mr. Big Shot. He went under a limb and was knocked off the horse Dad bought. He was so embarrassed. We all laughed as it was funny.

My brother John rode his horse, got off, and kicked it on its side and its hoof hit him in the face. We thought it killed him but it didn't. Lots of horse fun for us all.

* * *

We have talked about how bad my dad was. Now would like to tell some of his good points. When he was not drinking, he was great to be around. Mom would read to us out of Zane Grey's books and it was so enjoyable.

One time he took in three fellows to help them out. One was Pete Davis, Bob Hayes, Griffin Gardner called Sleepy. I think they stayed a year. Pete would run around and act like an ape. Dad always laughed as the guys were good-natured.

* * *

My mother's mother became ill and Mom had to go to Colorado and help her. Dad was left with us kids and I decided I would cook for him. I made cornbread but put in too much sugar and it tasted like cake. Dad didn't say a word and ate it, no fuss. I was glad he did not make me feel bad.

My grandmother died and Dad was good about watching us and taking care of everything until Mother came home. Instead of harsh, he was kind and good to us.

* * *

Many times when I was very young, kids would tease me at school because we did not have real nice clothes. This really hurt as there was nothing we could do to make things better. We did not have hot or cold water in the house. We also had an outhouse a ways from the house outside.

When we were little and company came, we had to sleep at the foot of the bed. (I believe there's a song about that.)

Our house had newspaper pasted on the walls. At night we would call to each other, boys to the girls and try to guess what we were looking at on the ceilings. To us this was game fun. We had kerosene lamps and a wood stove for heat. You might say we grew up the hard way.

I must tell you about our baby sister, Trula Gail. She was small and went to bed early. She would sleepwalk and come downstairs, eyes wide open and crawl into the wood box and all the time she was asleep. She did this often and we watched her close so she would not hurt herself.

* * *

Many winters our baby sister Trula Gail would get pneumonia. Marvin, a brother just four years older than I, we would run the two miles to town and back with medicine for her. Dad would be out drinking and so he was not there to take us. I'm sure her life was spared many times because of us running into town for the medicine.

* * *

My two older brothers went into the service. Melvin in the Navy and Kenny in the Air Force. They would send money home to help us live and Dad had 40 acres he bought and gave it to them when they got out of the service.

I was about 10 and my brothers would chase me with a garden snake. When they had a snake, I could always outrun them or so it seemed.

Leota was the oldest sister and she gave birth to a baby girl called Darlene. Leota was 15 when she had her. She ended up being the same age as our brother John. They really enjoyed playing together. Darlene saw John eating the butter out of the butter dish and she ran to my mother and told her John was going to get butter diabetes. Darlene hit John and made him cry. My mother said to Darlene, "What did you do that for?" She said, "But, Grandma, he was gonna hit me." Darlene later went to live with Mom and stepdad, Harry Baker.

My sister Leota had to comb my hair when I was younger. My hair was curly. She did not like to hear me scream when she put the comb through it. She took the scissors and gave me a boy Bob out of season. I have a picture of it even today and realized I did not look half bad. (First grade)

When I was in the first grade, I went out for recess and went downhill to pick a flower, near the school. I fell on some glass and cut a big gash in my arm. I still have the scar to this day. One of my classmate's sister took me to the doctor and they sewed it up.

* * *

There was a chiropractor doctor who lived a half mile up the road from us. His name was Walter Williams. His wife we called Auntie, and they had two children, Ivie, (nickname Mickey) her brother Dick or Dickie.

As we all grew up together, we would have measles together, mumps, flu, cold or whatever came at different times of the year. Such fun as they would stay with us and we would just be sick together.

Dickie would eat raw garlic and get on the school bus and we all got sick from the smell. His dad would say to us, you must eat raw garlic after going to the state fair. It would kill the bugs from whatever we ate. (Hold your nose!)

We, the Williams and the McEwens, were friends to the day they all died. I will see them in heaven someday.

Dickie died being a priest. Ivie died being a Mormon, she married Bill Collins from Winlock, Washington.

Auntie and Walter died in Puyallup, Washington. Where he remained a chiropractor.

* * *

At the age of nine or ten, I (Zoe) was offered a contract to be Shirley Temple's double. Mother and Dad would not accept as they felt the family was too large to go to California (Hollywood). Also Mom was Christian and did not believe in show business. My hair was long and curly at the time, also blonde.

* * *

While growing up on the home place, we had many interesting times. One time I was riding one of our horses. I thought I was a good rider, but one day was my last ride.

As I started to ride, the horse had a mind of its own and took off running a mile down the road to see some other horses. I would say this horse was high-spirited. Away we went and I could not control him. When he abruptly turned around and brought me back to a place across the street from our house. He stopped abruptly and off I went into the blackberry bushes. As I crawled out, I was pretty well scratched up. No more horses after this for me.

My older sister Gladys told me when she was 14 years old our father kicked her out of the house. She was on the street corner in Toledo, Washington crying when a neighbor came along and took her home with her. She lived there until she graduated. (Mrs. Layton)

My sister Lana Maude ran away to California when she was sixteen years old. Mom did not know where she was for a few years. I'm sure Mom was worried. Mom did not know if Lana was dead or alive.

We later found out she had married a man in the Navy in Oakland, California. Later she came back to Toledo with two little boys whom I babysat for as she worked in the restaurant in Toledo. I was twelve at this time in my life, and really thought I was grown up. After a year living with Lana, she moved back to Oakland to be with her husband. He had been discharged from the service.

* * *

When I was thirteen, and moved in and worked for the Richmans. They had a dairy farm and workers who lived in little cabins, helping milk the cows, and whatever went into running a farm. I would come home from school and help Lucille cook meals for everyone. They were like a family I never had at that time.

Because of Dad's meanness, he got rid of all of us at an early age. I was on the dairy farm until school was out and then home for the summer.

During the summer, I would often stay at Melvin and Lois's house and help put the hay in the barn. I only weighed 105 lbs. but I remember lifting bales of hay onto the truck.

I remember Dad always looked at us girls as guys on the home place. We worked like a man. I'm sure that's why we had bad backs later in life.

There were times I felt like a man in a woman's body. I dressed in jeans and had a boy's shirt. Later, you'll find out how God changed all that.

* * *

Before my folks divorced, my father had set up a sawmill on the home place. We, as children, were home part-time and I remembered peeling telephone poles for power lines. One thing, for sure, I became strong. Most of us girls had bad backs later in life from the hard work.

My mother was a godly woman and she had us go to church and many times we walked two miles into town and back. The church was Assembly of God and it was never my favorite church. I later went to the Presbyterian Church.

Dickie Williams the neighbor boy talked my younger brother John into using an umbrella and parachuting down into the hayloft. It was a distance and the umbrella went up as he went down. It almost broke his legs. Mom had her hands full raising all of us.

My brothers picked on me a lot, so Mom would put on the boxing gloves and go after them. We all thought it was great fun.

Brother John may be angry when he was milking the cows one morning so I threw a milk bucket at him, hitting him on his head. He still tells the story of me hitting him and it left a scar on his head. We were always told it was our Scotch/Irish temper not realizing it was pure anger.

* * *

When I was very small, I listened to the radio and was told as I grew older, I would yodel like on the radio. When people came to visit, they would have me yodel for everyone. Our family was quite musical. My mother's grandfather was a music teacher and had bright red hair.

I yodeled until I was about 20. The neighbors could hear me three or four miles away and knew I was out waiting for the bus to go to school.

When I first started preaching, they could not understand a loud voice coming out of a small lady. I was only one hundred and five pounds until I married in 1958 at the age of 26.

* * *

Mom could play almost any musical instrument and I'm sure it came (was inherited) from her Grandfather Oakley in England.

The neighbors would come to our house quite often to play instruments and sing songs. It was very Western. I grew up playing a guitar and singing at Western dances with the neighbor girl, Nora Cooper.

On weekends, the neighbors would come and we had ballgames and big dinners. I always hated it as I had to do the dishes afterward. Remember no hot or cold water in the house. We would have to heat the water to wash dishes.

My two older brothers loved to see me holler. They would pick on me and I would run down the road where Mom was quilting. Always before I could reach her, Melvin being tall would pick me up and take me back to the house screaming.

Later in life, I was always very close to Marvin and Melvin. Melvin's wife and I are still great friends to this day.

* * *

One of the things I enjoyed doing so much in my early teens and late, was to dance. Square dancing, ballroom dancing, jitterbug dancing, and just dancing. This habit stood between God and I for years.

* * *

Vision at age 16 (All night long it appeared I had cried.)

Growing up, I really did not believe in God or so I thought. At the age of sixteen, I had a night vision and this is how it went. In it, I was serving the Lord. At 16, I did not believe in God, Jesus, or hell.

Destruction had come to America. Wreckage was everywhere and few people left. In the vision dream, I was pulling people out from under the wreckage and putting them in a helicopter. I do not remember ever seeing a helicopter before this time.

As I did this I was crying, crying for joy as I knew the Lord was coming, but also crying for all who were lost or destroyed.

As I was busy helping to put people in a helicopter, the top three scriptures came to me at what was going on.

Isaiah 2:19 *And they shall go into the holes of the rocks, and into the caves of the earth for fear of the Lord, and for the glory of his majesty when he ariseth to shake terribly the earth.*

Isaiah 2:21 *To go into the cleft of the rocks into the top of the ragged rocks for fear of the Lord, and for the glory of his majesty and when he arises to shake terribly the earth.*

Revelation 6:14-17 *And the heaven departed as a scroll when it is rolled together; and every mountain and island were moved out of their places. And the kings of the earth, and the great men, and every bondman, and every free man, hid themselves in the dens and in the rocks of the mountain; and said to the mountains and rocks, fall on us, and hide us from the face of him that setteth on the throne, and from the wrath of the Lamb: for the great day of his wrath is come; and who shall be able to stand?*

I didn't know the Scriptures, as when I had them at sixteen, I was not a Christian. It showed God's hand on me before I was saved.

So all the more, I knew this vision was from the Lord. At the time this vision came to me, I would be a Christian when this came to pass. It is now 46 years later and nearing the time for this vision to come into being.

As we flew the people to the mountains tops by helicopter, I was made to know my husband was in the driver's seat.

All of a sudden Jesus stood in front of me and said, "After destruction to America, tell my people I'm coming immediately." Second ending: Just then Jesus appeared to me and said, "Tell my people I'm coming after destruction to America." I can still see Jesus so plain as though it was yesterday. (end of vision)

* * *

I left the Richman's dairy farm and moved into Toledo with the Williams for about a year. During this time, they helped me to become a lady. I had very little teaching on this. Ivie, their daughter, wore my clothes. We were just good sisters until the day she died. (Years later).

At sixteen, I moved into my own apartment over the hardware store. Worked at a soda fountain and burger bar for Cora Rockay and her husband Ray. Keeping up my schooling, all the while I was able to be one of the best dressed in high school.

While living over the Nash's hardware store, a group of young folks would get together on weekends and go bowling. So there was some fun along the way.

During this time living over the hardware store, I locked myself out of the apartment and had to get the police to get a ladder and crawl up to the window to get in. The folks in town teased me for weeks about this. In a small town, everyone knows everything that happens to you, or so it seemed.

* * *

You must be born again (September 1952)

This story really began when I was born into this world. The record shown here will be in 1948. It was in September just before school was to start. Hazel Bailey, a close friend of mine and I had been her bridesmaid, came to visit me.

Her husband went fishing and she had just gotten her driver's license and wanted me to go with her and her cousin Delores to Mossy Rock, Washington.

We were to follow her brother Jimmy Taylor who was driving a truck, so he could leave it there at his dad's lumber place. We had not seen each other for quite a while. So I begged Mom to let me go with them.

Reluctantly, she let me go as she didn't feel good about my going. Later we were to find out why.

Little did I know that day would be the beginning of life for me.

As we followed his little brother, Jimmy coming back from his dad's logging camp at Morton, Washington. His sister Jennifer was with them in the truck he was driving.

*   *   *

Hazel, Delores, and I were in the front seat of her car, following behind Jimmy. I was in the middle of the seat up front as we followed the truck.

Jimmy rounded a curve and it was a road with many curves. There'd been an accident in the road. Jimmy decided to stop abruptly. We came around the curve and instead of putting on her brakes, she accelerated into the back of the truck. I flew through the window and went the full length of the flatbed truck, hitting my head on the back of the truck. Had she swerved, we would have all been killed. Instead, we were all pretty badly hurt. I was close to death as it was.

I was told I went the full length of the flatbed truck hit my head into it. Also it took two or three men to hold me down in the car until he arrived at the hospital in Morton, Washington and then on to Tacoma General Hospital where I was for many weeks.

We were told they had to cut us out of the car. Hazel had her arm cut badly and Delores had two broken jaws, even as I did. Mine in four different places. Being in the middle, I received the full force. Face cuts (scars) were a few. Brain concussion, arm cut badly.

At the Morton hospital, a minister friend of our family who had known me all my life wanted to know who I was. I was so badly hurt, unrecognizable. He took glass out of my arm not knowing who I was at the time. My leg was hurt badly also. Mom and Dad arrived and were quite concerned. Mom had, had a premonition something bad was going to happen. She had reluctantly let me go that day with Hazel.

They then took me to the Tacoma General Hospital where I was lingering between life and death for over three or four days. Mother stayed by my bedside praying and having the church pray. Later I learned she and God made a covenant about my life. Thank God for a praying mother.

As she and God were making a covenant, I was being taken into heaven and hell. He let me know I was on my way to hell and asked me if He gave me another chance would I accept Him and serve Him and preach the gospel.

I didn't want to go to hell as it was really bad. I saw people cursing, living a bad life, and everyone so miserable.

The Lord showed me if I would serve Him with all my heart and life He would let me live and do so. He wanted me to show others how to be saved.

I also remember God showed me every strange thing that happened to me in my life up until then and why.

For an example, when in first grade and second grade the crowd turned against a girl in our classroom. She was like I was, could not dress nice so she had no nice clothes to dress in. I stood up against the crowd for her. I had a close friend and I warned her if she went with the crowd, she would never be my friend again. She went the way of the crowd and I did not let her in close to me again. Until later in life. She went through many hard times because of the life she chose.

Later in life, when we did connect again, she let me know she was sorry. She made the bad choice, the bad decision. She had many heartaches until later in life.

Note: Additional details about injury from the accident

I was hurt badly. Also my face scarred badly. I was in a coma for five days or more. After this, five doctors came and told my mother, there was nothing more they could do for me.

While in the coma, the Lord Jesus came to visit me and showed me heaven and hell. He let me know I was on my way to hell. I knew this also because I never accepted Him as my personal Savior.

Mother continued with the doctors to keep trying and she said God had placed a call of God on my life by my mother.

While still in a coma, God gave me a choice of preaching His gospel and serving Him. I said yes and He healed me. And I came out of the coma. Went home in three weeks. They had thought six months. The brain surgeon said he went into the back of my nose put a piece of skin into place, allowing me to come out of the coma. While in the coma, I could hear what the five doctors said. I could not let anyone know I was hearing as I could not move. I believe people in comas can hear because I did.

The reason God had to show me this was so when I became a Christian I would stand firm in Him. It's always easy to go the way of the crowd, but hard sometimes to stand firm on your conviction.

Also God let me know why I went through all these trials and felt as though I was a misfit in life.

In my teens, I had asked to get in the car accident and die, as I felt I did not belong in this world. Hebrews 11:13.

Later in the Word, I found out we are not of this world. No wonder the world did not want to receive us. God has chosen me from my mother's womb and is it any wonder my life should be a strange one.

I also understand the scripture in John 15:6, "You have not chosen me, I have chosen you and ordained you, that you should go and bring forth much fruit, and your fruit should remain: that whatever, you shall ask the father in my name, He may give it to you."

* * *

Back at the hospital and with my mother, five doctors came into the room and said there was no hope for me. My mother said they must keep trying that she was praying and knew God was going to heal me. I could hear them talking though I was in a coma. I wanted to tell them I'd had an experience with the Lord and said yes, I would serve Him and preach the gospel wherever He wanted to take me.

The doctor said it would be a miracle if I lived. The brain surgeon went in and pressed a piece of skin back into place that had been mis-lodged. Then I came out of the coma and all five doctors gave God the credit.

I left the hospital in three weeks and they thought it would be six months or so. There were 12 long weeks in bed at home. I had terrible migraine headaches. My weight had gone from 105 pounds to 86 pounds. For over a year, I could only eat through a tube as my jaws were broken in four different places and wired shut.

* * *

Friends I was not allowed to have because they would make me laugh and it hurt me. So wires were all over in my teeth. I spent over two or three months in the dentist often getting my teeth pulled.

I had to get the upper teeth pulled and received an upper denture. Also later a lower partial.

When I could, I went to school to see my friends. I remember Bessie Sherman fainted when she saw me. I'm sure I looked bad, but really was glad to see them all. (What an experience!)

I'd wanted to quit school until this happened to me, then I realized how important a diploma is in order to get a good job. It ended up I took two semesters in one and got an A and B winning a scholarship to be a nurse. I ended up not taking it as I could not stand the sight of blood.

But this time I recovered enough to get a job at a restaurant in town and made good money while still in school.

* * *

While at home getting well at Mom's, one morning woke up and found the wires in my mouth had broken. This was bad as we were afraid my jaws which had been painfully set would move and I'd have to have the jaws set again. My mother took me to the dentist and they rewired them and all turned out well. To this day, we did not know what caused the wires to break.

Another funny thing that happened while I was recovering from all this, Mom was mopping the floor and the cat come into the house. Mother made a dash to get it out, and as she did, she slipped and down she went. I thought she was hurt bad, so I jumped out of bed to go help her. It ended up she had to carry me back to bed. It is strange how we react to circumstances, is it not?

* * *

After graduation, I moved into a house with the three Stanfield girls: Hilda, Freda and Laura we called Punky. We all worked at the same restaurant in town. We were together possibly a year or so. Then I left the town of Toledo and moved to Seattle, Washington where I got a job at Boeing. Had an apartment in a women's home and caught the bus back and forth from work. I enjoyed it very much.

Recently at 90, Hilda went to be with the Lord. Freda also passed away this last year. Punky is still alive and many of her family. The Stanfields are one of the families we had ballgames with and big dinners.

Remember I had to wash the dishes such fun. Ha!

* * *

When I was seventeen, I met Bill Bolar and we went together until he went into the service and was sent to Korea for three years. We corresponded and made plans to marry, but God had other plans for my life. Remember God called me to serve Him while in a coma.

I went with Bill until after I graduated from high school. We planned to marry when he came home. When I had my second experience with God and really gave my heart to God and got salvation, water baptism and the works. When Bill returned home, things were different. I found out he'd been cheating on me with an old girlfriend.

One night as his folks' house when I spent the night, God really dealt with me to give him up. He wrote on the wall with his finger and said, "If I married him, I would end up on Skid Row."

You see by this time God had dealt with me to go to Bible school and I had planned to go. Bill and I broke up and he married the girl he cheated on me with.

Later years, I found out his wife and her mother died and went to heaven. I have never been sure about Bill if he made it. Someday I shall see Bill's mother and sister made heaven. I'm still in touch with Perry Watkins, her husband, who was in the Army and spent much time in Germany. He really liked it over there. He was a demolitions expert and it was strange as he was colorblind.

* * *

Marvin, a brother just older than I, when he was young, he drove cars for Bill Gates' dad – Bill Gates from Microsoft. His father was a Christian, I believe at that time.

When Marvin was young, he went to Alaska with my older brother Kenny and his wife Betty. After Alaska, Marvin went into the Army.

* * *

I'm speaking of this brother Marvin as I was leaving Boeing on a leave of absence for year to go and helped he and his wife in Virginia. He married a girl from Ireland and had two daughters together. I worked in a drugstore in Virginia. I came back to Washington with them, when they were expecting their first daughter, Linda.

The trip itself was quite an experience as a child in the convertible. I was shown we would be in an accident and when we came to Bend, Oregon, it happened. There was ice on the road and we hit a patch of it. It turned the car upside down in the ditch. Dorothy was eight months pregnant and she somehow landed outside the car on the snow. My brother was thrown back on me in the back seat.

A truck was behind us. He told us it was like a big hand was underneath us and it hit down as light as a feather. God was protecting us for sure. We went to the hospital in Bend, Oregon and we were all okay. My brother had a slight concussion but God had healed him as I laid hands on him and prayed for him. At this time, they both were not Christians.

After the accident with Marvin and wife in Bend, Oregon, I came back to Washington and went back to work at Boeing until I decided to go to Bible school.

* * *

I believe I mentioned I broke up with my boyfriend Bill Bolar and God had given me a vision of me ending up on Skid Row if I married him. God showed me a writing on the wall by the Lord's finger showing me what would happen if I married him.

I thought of going to Canada to the Presbyterian Bible school, but God had other plans for me.

One night I came home from work and received a phone call from a girlfriend in my hometown of Toledo, Washington.

She called my mother and got my number as God had spoken to her about me coming to Portland where she was going to Bible school.

I quit Boeing and was on a new adventure. During the two years, I learned much. After my money ran out, I helped cook for the school. Then I got a job at JJ Newberry's making sandwiches. My how God began to talk to me and give me many revelations.

After taking the job at JJ, I had to walk two miles to work. I had to pray I would not get rained on. I met a little Gypsy girl and she wanted to tell me my fortune.

She looked at the palm of my hand and said she saw the Star of David. Then I told her I would tell her, her fortune. She said she believed I could. I really could not.

Another time I was walking back to school, it was dark. A young man overtook me and asked why I was out so late. I told him I did not have money for a bus and had to believe God to take care of me. He then volunteered to walk me home to be safe. We stopped at a restaurant and had hot chocolate, his treat. Out of this friendship, I led him back to the Lord and helped him buy clothes to return home as a well-dressed man. God is so good.

Also while walking the two miles to the school, I met a family called the Campbells. They lived on Eighth Street in Portland, Oregon. A group of us from college would go visit with them and they would fix us homemade biscuits and gravy. During the two years there in school, I led the whole family to the Lord. We're still friends to this day.

* * *

The Lord had spoken to me that I was going to get a call and that was where I was to go. I did not question it because God had spoken to me about the call.

Let's go back and I will tell you how I truly became a born-again believer. When I worked at Boeing, a lady I met from my hometown came to see me. We went dancing and I found she was a wild one. While in the nightclub as a voice spoke to me and said, "You are going to get saved." I'd had my first experience in a coma. This was to be my next experience and I finally made it.

I listened to a radio broadcasting station and it said soldiers and sailors were getting saved. So I said, "Why not me?"

* * *

God spoke to me when I was in Portland before I left for the ministry. I'm going to give you the five-fold ministry in your life. The nine gifts of the Spirit and whatever you have need of to bring deliverance to people. And I said, "How can You do that?"

He said if I am in you, I am all nine gifts of the Spirit, I am all nine fruits of the Spirit, and I am the five-fold ministry. He is everything you have need of, for miracle after miracle after miracle. He is the miracle God.

When I was getting ready to leave Wings of Healing, I found out that the minister running the school was not a Christian at all. This I found out as I led one of his prostitutes to the Lord. This minister had taken money from people coming to school there and instead of sending them to the mission field, they were kicked out without getting their money back. He owned a big building in Portland downtown and he ran the prostitution house. Sad, sad.

He finally, after we left, moved to Los Angeles, California. We had collected enough to put him in jail for life but he was too crooked and had a way out. Sad, sad.

Leaving the school, I stayed at Bill and Judy Bennett's house and prayed and studied for a whole year. Then proceeded to go to Africa to the mission field. God had spoken to me about going to Memphis and I made plans through Mrs. Purvis Lane to stay at her sister's.

As I got ready to leave, God said I was to leave on Thursday. I had $0.10 in my pocket. I went to a church there in Portland and met Don Ducan, whom I had gone to school with.

I told him I was leaving Thursday for Memphis, Tennessee. He told me he was leaving that day also to see his dad who lived close to Oakland, California. My sister lived there. So we went to his dad, spent the night, and he took me to my sister's.

Bill and Judy whom I had led to the Lord while in Bible school said they would pay for the bus fare from Oakland to Memphis. During this time of getting ready to leave, over $300 came in to help me on my trip from friends and relatives.

Arriving in Memphis, I had many good experiences. While staying at Thelma's sister's house I babysat a little boy who was driven by demon spirit. I was able to cast it out and he became normal. His mom wanted to give him to me but at the time could not.

About this time, I had a dream I was going down the highway at 100 miles an hour. I saw a white Stetson hat so I stopped to pick it up. When I picked it up, it had beer cans and tobacco in it. Then I proceeded.

When arriving in Memphis, Tennessee I stayed at Thelma Lane's sister's home. She did not charge me for rent for the room and it gave me time to keep close to the Lord.

I would attend Dr. Paul Grubb's church where I met many wonderful people. These include Bill Britton and his wife Nadine whom I became very close to.

I prophesied a lot during the three months I was there. Many things had happened in the church and God allowed me to help straighten things out. I met Tom Hamilton, Sr. and he introduced me to his mother, Rosadell. His mom lived in Texarkana, Arkansas. She and I traveled around a bit together. We all gathered around Paul Grubbs as he was getting ready to go to the West Indies. He had a Bible school and one of his teachers was Bill Britton. We all gathered around and no one gave the prophecy I gave to him.

Maybe they were afraid as he was the head pastor of the school. The prophecy went like this:

You will go to the West Indies and take down with heart attack, which happened. You are to tell the men you are with they are to hold you up in prayer and you will through it, which happened. Then you will start a revival throughout the West Indies and he did. That happened as spoken. Then I told him I had more to tell him when he got back. By this time, he was almost afraid of me.

I also told him I had more to tell him when I got back home from Kansas City and it was good. Needless to say he became a friend of mine which he should not have.

She and I were getting ready for a trip to Kentucky. Before we left, I felt I must talk to Paul Grubbs. I was able to corner him and tell him the rest of the prophecy God had given me. You are persecuted. Many preachers as they come through as they were trying to show you some new revelation. God was revealing and that God wanted him to wait on the Lord as God was fixing to give him new revelation.

I told him he knew the Word backwards and forwards but needed to spend more time on his knees and God would show him updated things and his church would fill up again and he would be blessed. This did take place.

Our trip to Kentucky started out. We were to be at a meeting in Kansas City, Missouri. A young fellow I went to Bible school with was there. It was New Year's night and ever so noisy.

As we were traveling up to Kansas City, we were a hundred miles from there and close to being out of gas. We forgot to fill the tank and we drove on an empty tank into Kansas City, Missouri. (Miracle, yes) The greatest miracle of it all was we had angels all over our car and a dove came over the window. And, of course, we ran on an empty gas tank for 100 miles. (Miracle, yes.)

Down the highway at a lesser speed, all of a sudden the road became winding and I realized by stopping to pick the hat up it saved my life. Had I been going at the fast speed, I could've killed myself. I came around a curve and there was a graveyard. I was made to know I would have been in the graveyard.

I met Bill Britton and his family at Paul Grubbs Bible college and church. I prophesied in the church for the three or so months I was there. Bill Britton helped me get meetings all through the South. I preached in many churches and had a good time with the Brittons.

One church in Arkansas, I went to pray for a man. When I came to, I was on the other side of church wondering how I got there. The people said I did a Charleston dance like I was floating on air. I had said if true revival was there, I would dance. Marvelous experience. While in Grubbs' church, he was getting ready to go to the West Indies, the Lord had me give him this prophecy.

After the Saturday meeting, we left for Kentucky. After arriving there we found out it was the school of prophets and they did not believe in women ministers. A large group came and we ended up having a meeting in the parking lot.

From Kentucky, we went to Texas to pray for Pastor Cole who was dying. We were not allowed to get into pray for him and he did die.

We really did learn a lot there. God never sends you to do something and others cause it to not come to pass.

When Rosadell and I got back from Kentucky, he began to tell me what God had shown him. As a result, as I was getting ready to leave Memphis and go to Syracuse, New York, he prophesied over me and said I was a prophetess.

Leaving Memphis and on to Syracuse, New York where I was in a meeting for two weeks. Much took place during this time.

* * *

I had taken my shots and my arm was sore. I thought, why couldn't I fly? God said, "No. This will happen on the bus. Many things will happen on the bus and it's ordained of Me. You will lead many souls to Christ."

We left for the bus depot and I didn't even have enough for a bus ticket. But when you live by faith, you knew God would provide.

Two ladies I had met at church each gave me $12=$24. The ticket was $30 or more. I had five dollars on me and when I picked up my mail, my aunt had sent just what I needed for my ticket. I fasted a lot so I did not worry about eating.

As we started, we traveled all night and on the bus I had chance to witness to everyone including the bus driver. They were telling dirty jokes and one fellow came up and asked me what I did. I told him I was going as a missionary to Africa. Next thing I knew they were all around me asking questions. I told them all how to get saved. The bus driver was a Christian. He said, "Miss McEwen, that was God." The bus driver was praying with Zoe all the time.

The next morning, a married couple asked if they could treat me to breakfast and I said yes, as I did not have any money.

Next experience, the Lord had shown a young man and I would sit next to him and he could not get out of his seat. I do not remember his name but the Lord had me tell him through a word of knowledge about his life. Zoe said she had a message for the young man from God. He said, "Don't talk to me about God." Zoe said, "I have to deliver it and if you get mad, you get mad." I said your two older sisters are looking for you as they all had been adopted out. And when you get where you're going, they will be there. Also the Lord told me that he had been living with a Catholic family and they had "religioned" him. He had been religioned to death. And the young man would get angry as he would talk about it. This time he listened and I led him to the Lord. No wonder God didn't want me to go by plane.

In Buffalo, New York he asked me if he could treat me to lunch and the Lord said it was okay. When I went to the ladies room, he bought me a bracelet and put $20 in the box. Told me not to open it until I got to Syracuse, New York. I kept in touch with them for quite some time. Then lost touch.

Another glimpse of a Zoe adventure ...

After the young couple had found me and fed me, I went to Cleveland, Ohio where Bill Britton had set it up for me to minister in the church there ran by the Beattys. I got lost on the way to the church and came in late. It had been snowing. They did not have boots for my feet or a scarf. My head was so cold.

As I came through the door, a prophecy was being given and it said, "I have provided boots for your feet and a warm shawl for my head and money to continue my journey." What a blessing that was. Good things took place in the meeting.

The Beattys gave me their folks' address so when I would arrive in New York I'd have some place to go. As I traveled, God opened many doors for me to minister. Then after Ohio, proceeded on to Syracuse, New York.

Buffalo, New York   Albany, New York   Syracuse, New York

What God had shown me. Many healings and deliverance went on there. Unusual things happened, one in particular. A man came forth to have me pray he would quit smoking, only instead I told him to take the brace off his leg as he was defrauding the government.. He fell out under the power of God and hit the cement floor. I did not hurt him, but it scared me as I was new in ministry, and it had never happened before.

In Syracuse, New York, was quite an interesting time. Stayed at the Shanks home. Ivie was my roommate in Bible school and it was her grandmother's home. And we went into meeting there, the pastor always distanced himself from me probably because I had a word of knowledge. God would show me all about what was going on in the church. The pastor at that time had deceived the young people into being loose in their lives. He was using them in a way very unpleasing to the Lord. I asked Evie's grandmother who was in charge of the church and she said she was. So I proceeded to tell her what was going on.

She said she was going to take care of it. Zoe suggested that she speak with the teenagers about what was going on. By the time I left Grandma's, she had checked with some of the teenagers and found out what I said was true.

Back to the pastor, no names mentioned, he left the church within two and a half weeks, after Ivie's grandmother exposed everything.

God told me to love him. God says to love your enemies and those who despitefully use you.

The pastor knew I had gone to the Bible school in Portland and had exposed it for what it was. The man who ran the Bible school when I was there was crooked and we had enough evidence to put him in prison for life but it went as far as Washington DC. And I'll leave it there.

He bound the meeting so I told the people they might as well go home as he had decided to bind the meeting. Then the pastor stood to his feet and confessed he was the man. He released the meeting and God did His job and we had a great meeting. Many deliverances, healings, etc. After all left, we went with the pastors home and I really let him have it for not having the discernment he should have had.

Later he scheduled a meeting for me at his church in Brooklyn. Brother Sweet had booked my meeting for me and I was not too pleased with this man.

I visited Elm Bible Institute. Met the Wilhelms' sister and brother-in-law of Ivie Shank, my roommate at Bible school in Portland. We had good fellowship and exchanged revelations God had shown through the years.

* * *

As you know, I was on my way to Africa. Dr. Sweet took me to downtown New York and introduced me to the headman over twelve Episcopalian churches in New York City. The minister and Dr. Sweet I trusted to help me get my vision to go to Africa. They found out too many white women were marrying black men and they would not give me my visa as I was not married and they felt it would be too dangerous for me. I was to be in SJ Elton's Bible school in Nigeria.

I was at a meeting one night and a prophecy came to me saying I was to return to the West Coast – Portland, Oregon to minister.

I kept the date in 1957 in Brooklyn New York with this man (no name) and fulfill the obligation of the meeting. This man was still testing me to see if I was of God.

So he put his wife in back of the church, fur coat and all. Where she looked like a wealthy lady. But I was not fooled. I called her out and told her she was the wife of a traveling evangelist and because of her prayers and staying home, God had blessed them. Also I asked her to help me minister in the meeting and she did and we did, and the meeting was great. This was in 1957. Billy Graham was in New York ministering.

We had about 1,000 that night to my surprise. One man came in one night and I told him all about his wife and he gave his heart to the Lord. We had many miracles and deliverances. When the meeting was over, I left to come back to Portland, Oregon as God had spoken.

I stayed all night at a black folks' home. They treated me royally. They fixed up two or three big sacks of food as I was going traveling by train. I could never have eaten all they gave me but I knew God had a purpose for it.

Sure enough refugees were on the train and I was able to help feed them as they only had one meal a day. Thank God for those black folks who listened to God. What a blessing they were.

Many miracles and blessings in this church. While at Evie's grandmother's house, I met Ivie's sister and her husband from Bible school. After leaving Syracuse, New York proceeded on to New York City came in by bus to downtown New York where the Beattys' folks lived. They ran a design shop for clothes. They were leaving on a missionary trip and so went with me to the bus depot.

In Brooklyn, I picked up my baggage. They gave me $20 and called a cab and paid for me to go out to Long Island, New York. Here I stayed at Brother William's church. He had a prophet or prophetical room. They were very lovely and I traveled out to many places from their church.

One unusual thing happened when I was there. God spoke to me to go to Maryland and give a young man a warning he was marrying the wrong girl. I did not have the money to go on and a couple at the church said God told them to give me their vacation money. It pays to be obedient. I left for Maryland and gave the young man the message. Never did hear how it turned out.

Coming back from Maryland, I was going to the church at Long Island and saw a gang forming on the street corner. God said go give them a gospel tract. I walked forward then with my suitcase and did as I was told to. They started making fun of me but two girls came down and started talking to me. They had just been to the Billy Graham Crusade and had had an experience. Next, the other one picked up my suitcase and carried it to the church and the service was letting out. The priest walked up as most of them went to the Catholic school and his church. After this took place, they never stood out as a gang again. And they would holler and wave at me, when I was out and about.

From Long Island, I went out and ministered many places. When I arrived in Long Island, I went to service with the Williams. The man that spoke that night told us he was scheduled to speak elsewhere but God had him cancel and come and speak at this meeting. It was strange but wonderful as he had a message for me.

I traveled for the whole year and all of a sudden, the enemy hit me with doubt that God would meet my needs. That is what he ministered on, God would meet my needs and before I left the meeting that night, two or three people placed $20 or more in my hands. Very encouraging it was.

Was invited to minister in Bangor, Maine at Brother so-and-so, can't remember his name but can remember vividly what happened that week I was there. When I traveled, I fasted a lot and was ready for every challenge. On arrival, the church I stayed in the pastor's home because I was single he would work with me as I ministered to people.

A young lady in the church had been believing for deliverance and the first night I began to cast out spirits and I got to one I had never heard of before. So I stopped and commanded all the spirits to be bound until I could figure out what to do.

After the meeting was over, I asked the pastor if there was a spirit like that. He said yes.

The pastor and I went out to her house and dealt with it privately. I told them the following Sunday I would cast it out, call it an unclean spirit, and she was to release it as she knew I knew what it was. On Sunday, her father came to church with her and as she was delivered and filled with the Holy Ghost, her father gave his heart to the Lord. He said it's the first time in all her life she had smiled. Last I heard, she went out as a missionary.

Another episode at this church was seven or eight young people came in the church and started shimmying up the aisles. Deep from within me came a rebuke in tongues. I told them to just take a seat like everyone else.

One of the young ladies had at one time been their youth leader but was talked into going into a false cult. Believing in free love. I prayed for her and she was set free as I told them all about the occult they were in. Also through a word of knowledge, the Lord made it plain, He was closing the door on the church where they went. She went back and told them all that I said. In two weeks, the church closed.

Connecticut

After leaving Maine, it was winter time and it reminded me of Washington where I lived most of my life.

The next place I ministered at was at Durham Center, Connecticut. The Rev. Sweet was pastor, he also was the head of the Full Gospel in New York City.

They had a little chapel there where he ministered a month or so. Also in Hartford, Connecticut. There was a professor that came to a home meeting I was in one night. This night was very unusual as the Lord took over my body and ministered through me. When it was over, they told me it was the best they had ever heard. I sure didn't do nothing except let God speak through me.

Also ministered in an auditorium and the little girl came up to me after the meeting and told me she saw Jesus with His hand on my back. I knew He was there but did not know anyone could see Him. Oh the faith of a little child.

While ministering in Durham Center one night, a man came from Brooklyn, New York. The Lord showed me he was coming and he did not.

When at Durham Center., Connecticut, a man came early in the morning to talk to me about his problems. God had shown me the day before he was coming. This is what God had me tell him. He had a bad temper and the judge had told his attorney if he didn't bite his tongue and be still, he was going to put him in jail. So I told him to be quiet and not get angry or mad and be still. When he went before the judge, he marveled at his attitude and he told his attorney he had been ready to send him to jail for a month.

The end result, he came into God and his life totally changed. Thank God for the word of knowledge.

Another thing I will bring out at this time, while ministering one time God gave me an address and I went there and the people were waiting for me. We had a marvelous meeting. I never knew them and they did not know me. But God showed them I was coming.

For the six months I ministered up in the East, God revealed to me the Sons of God ministry. I could hear a conversation one thousand miles away. Sort of like Superman. He would show me what happened in the meeting ahead of time. If I have written this before, it bears repeating again. A man came to me and said he had a criminal mind and wanted it changed. That night Jesus stepped into my body and I saw Jesus take his mind and change it around. Later he told me, his mind was different.

Also a young lady came to my meeting. She was an RN nurse and had a disease that only God could change. Like this young man the Lord stepped into my body and healed her completely.

The Story Continues

The Story Continues...

I came back from New York in 1957 and God led me to go to California with Dorothy Wood, a girl I went to Bible school with. Her mother was the best cook ever and had cooked in restaurants. She led the singing and I preached. We visited a Bible school in L.A. and they did teach us how to witness to Jews.

When we arrived at the Bible school, we waited and one of the ministers came down to welcome us, and put us up at the home of the young man who at that time played piano and organ for the Lawrence Welk show. From there after a week, we went on to San Bernardino, California. My uncle was there and we went to an Assembly of God church to minister.

I turned God loose with the gifts of the spirit and word of knowledge. There was a lady there and she was in a wheelchair. I told her if she would visit a lady she was at odds with, God would heal her. She acknowledged she had ought against her and said she would do it. The pastor did not agree with me and closed the meeting down. This did not stop God. The lady did as I told her to and was healed. It started a revival in the homes of people from that church. He went to my uncle's church and held a revival for a few weeks. Then was led to return back to Portland.

Dorothy and I went to some youth meetings in homes where we met a lot of people our own age. I met Jack Hodgdon, and introduced him to his wife. His wife's in heaven but we are still in touch.

During these meetings, I was to meet Paul. God had given me a vision of a man with black hair and a son with strawberry blond hair. I kidded everyone and said if they knew anyone like that introduce me. So two of the guys from our meetings brought Paul and that's how I met him.

I stayed at Bill and Judy Bennett's house when I was in Portland. Soon after meeting Paul, he did some missionary work in Mexico. Possibly two months. When he returned, we were invited to teach in a Bible camp at Big Bear, California. He was with the guys and I was with the girls. It turned out to be a great thing to do.

When I was twenty-five, I ministered in Sammy's church in Vancouver, Washington. He allowed me to let whoever God sent in and showed me, he was to give the message that night. I would let them minister.

There was a lady in his church in a wheelchair. She thought I was the one to pray the prayer of faith for her and she would be healed. But God revealed to me, I would not be the one praying for her.

This one night a Brother Bradley came into the meeting, and I called him up and told him he was to preach. He acknowledged it and said God sent him. He preached a faith message and in the middle of his message, he spoke to the lady in the wheelchair to come up out of her seat. She did and was miraculously healed. She danced all over the church with her eyes closed and never hit anyone.

Years later, in Auburn, Washington, a lady by the name of Mable Bowen and daughter came to live in my sister's apartments in Algona, Washington. Her daughter was pregnant out of wedlock.

There was a meeting going on at the Indian reservation. The same man who had preached in my meeting years before was the one speaking at the reservation.

Redding, California: Uncle's Church 1955

I worked in my uncle's church for a year or so. He was schooling me about my gifts and let me preach and go out and pray for people with him. There was a Presbyterian minister who was very ill and they thought he would die. I heard about it and asked my uncle to go with me and let the church know our church was praying for him. As a result, he was healed. He sent one of his elders to my uncle's church to see how we believed.

He came in, sat in the back, and my uncle gave a prophecy and spoke in tongues. Then uncle said there was no need for an interpretation as someone got the message. This Presbyterian elder took my uncle's elder outside and said is that what you call speaking in tongues? And the elder said yes. He said I got the message as I understood the language. This elder took it back to the Presbyterian church and they began to believe in it.

It was at my uncle's church I met Bud and Fran Schillinger and we were friends for life.

Our Marriage

After meeting Paul, my husband to be, we went to David Shock's camp meeting and counseled the youth at Big Bear Lake in California. David wrote the song, "His Name is Wonderful." (Prince of Peace, Mighty God, the Everlasting Father. I'm sure there was more to it but it was the theme of the camp meeting.)

Not long after the camp meeting, Paul went to Mexico to minister. He took Tony Nuevo with them to Guadalajara where they were in ministry. After meeting Paul, a year later we married and stayed a while in Portland and later moved to Tacoma, Washington where Paul started work at Boeing. John Hamilton, Rosadell's son, also came up nearby and worked at Boeing.

God give me a vision of my husband before I met him. He had a little boy named Dan. I met Paul when Dan was two and half years old. I fell in love with Paul's son first and we married when he became three and a half years old.

Paul and I dated for a year and had fourteen prophecies Paul was the one I should marry. Up until now I had many offers but none God had said was the one. We were to be tried on this after we married but God always knows best.

We married September 29, 1958, and a year later had a baby girl, Lelia. Dan was so glad to have a sister.

I was 26 when we got married and Paul was three years older than I. We married in Portland, Oregon and then moved to Tacoma where Paul worked at Boeing. Also I was pregnant with Lelia. Two weeks later, she was born in the Tacoma hospital.

During my pregnancy, I was very ill and almost lost Lelia. When carrying Lelia, I hemorrhaged hard enough to lose her. But had a vision of her in God's hands and the next day I became better. When she was born, she was only five pounds and was quite sickly. She was allergic to penicillin, even to this day. God spoke and said each of my children would be a miracle and they were.

I spent a good part of seven months in bed. One of the funny things that happened to Danny and I was we had flying bugs come out the floor and I had to send him upstairs in the apartment house to get the owner to come vacuum them out. I could not get out of bed to do anything. The manager came and sucked them up with the vacuum cleaner. We had to move to another apartment while he put in a new floor.

Another cute thing Dan did was he went from apartment to apartment and asked if they wanted to get saved. Most were Jehovah Witnesses and they thought he was cute. He was four years old at this time. Had a little red fire engine and rang his bell and asked people if they wanted to get saved and accept Jesus as their personal savior. He had a little Bible and was ready to tell them how.

Met a lady Christian in real estate and she rented us a house in Burien, Washington. Sixteen months later, I had Diane. I laid in bed five months with her and when she was born the cord was wrapped around her neck. She was blue at birth.

Our family began and through it I was sick having them. They were very much wanted.

We met some folks by the name of Winecoops from Idaho. They prayed for me twice and God showed him I would have a miracle. Diane was born one day before her big brother Dan's birthday 18th and 19th of February. Our older son Dan loved that he had two sisters to pick on and tease.

Must say, six years later a lovely son came to our house. He was born a miracle and a man of God. Prayed for him and God healed him of a twisted intestine. A prophecy came that he would be a prophet and he is now 50 years old. God revealed much to him. We are so grateful for our family of four.

Tim was a great miracle as he didn't come to birth until 10 months I carried him. They pulled him out of me with forceps and just missed his heart. He still has marks to this day.

Seven months in bed to have Lelia, five months in bed to have Diane. Each child I had was a miracle and so loved by us. Dan the oldest son has been a great blessing to us. He has a lovely family, son, and twin daughters. How blessed he is. Also a lovely wife. At this time, I have nine grandchildren and 11 great grands. God has blessed us so much.

Paul and I had two daughters. They were like two peas in a pod, sixteen and a half months apart. When I dressed them, they liked the same dresses, same doll, etc. Only the oldest had black hair like her dad, Paul. The youngest had blonde hair and blue eyes. My mother had blue eyes and one of my grandmothers, if not both, had blue eyes. Needless to say, they were both beautiful babies.

As the children grew up, we would be out on the back porch and all the neighbor kids gathered (or on the front porch depending on the house we were in). I would always get a chance to witness to them all about our Lord and Savior Jesus Christ.

In the girls' teens, they would ask for money to buy their clothes and I would give it to them. They would go out separately and buy the same dress but a different color. I found this very interesting.

The girls learned from neighbors how to crochet, knit, cook. I taught them to clean house. Having to drive long distances to work, I missed going to their school affairs. I could not help with their homework. The teachers would pick on them and I would defend them. I would let them know they should be able to teach them without my help as they could cook, clean house, etc. I did end up hiring a tutor and a graduated with high honors. I was always proud of them.

The Lord had me listen to what they said. In Phoenix, one morning they got up to go to school, Diane and Tim both had a dream of a tornado coming toward our house. After they left for school, the tornado was coming toward our house. I commanded it to go down in South Phoenix and it did. As I spoke, it took off commercial building roofs but hurt no one.

We moved to Auburn, Washington in 1972. There were no jobs at the time so we had to move into a house which God had given me a vision of and all the bad things I would go through in this house.

This house was haunted. One lady, Alma McClure, saw 125 hippie spirits in the house. Two poltergeist spirits were there most of the time. One a child that tap danced and threw a ball down the stairs. The older man, possibly the little girl's grandfather, walked up and down the stairs, and out on the porch up and down.

There was a Filipino man who raised berries commercially in a big garden on his land not far from our house. Since we had no jobs yet, we helped him save his berries. Also helped in the garden.

While in Burien, we met Dick and Connie Beck and became good friends throughout the years. We saw our children grow up together and was there when Dick died and made sure he knew God. Also was there when Connie went home to be with the Lord. She had a wonderful mom whom I loved much; from the old school. God is God and there is no doubt about it. A great godly woman. Try to keep in touch with her children even now but it is hard.

Dan, our oldest son

After graduation from Tucson University, Dan was chosen out of a thousand to be a pharmacist. There were only forty chosen. He went to Long's drugstore in California.

Before going to work at the drugstore, Dan decided to go swimming at the Wedge in Costa Mesa, California. Here he was slammed into the Wedge and broke his neck. We received word it was very bad and I was not working at the time. I went to be with him. The doctor said he would have to wear a halo around his neck, maybe for the rest of his life. We believed in miracles I told the doctor that. He said he had been in business for thirty years and it would have to be a miracle.

Paul and Pat Wasielewski knew a lovely Catholic family near the hospital and I stayed two weeks. They were so good to me and took me back and forth to the hospital.

When I was there, his fever went down. When I came home for the night, it went up. The doctor was able to get it very close to perfect, the first miracle he said.

The nurses put perfume in the room as he smelled like seaweed. They rotated him around and they tried to get it cleaned off him.

While with this special family, I went to church with them. And the church was Holy Ghost-filled nuns and priests. It was a wonderful place to worship the Lord.

After three or so months, God did heal our son's neck and he went to work for Long's drug company.

When I first arrived, I called his boss and asked him to come by and assure Dan his job would be okay. So he could get well. He did come by and brought games and encouraged him a great deal. After my son recovered, he went to Aspen, Colorado staying with him and they were friends.

At this time in life, our son Dan has a lovely home, wife, children, two girls and a boy in Windsor, California. To know the rest of the story he will have to write his own book. P.S. I fasted the full two weeks with no food, just water.

* * *

Some unusually funny things that happened when the children were gone. Dan, our oldest, was in the sixth grade and I was at home praying. The Lord gave me a vision of him on the school grounds telling dirty jokes and cussing up a storm. The Lord spoke to me and said when he gets home tell him the Lord saw him on the school grounds doing what he did. He told me not to scold him. The Lord wanted him to know the Lord saw what he was doing. He said, "Mom, I was doing it, too."

Another time Dan was in eighth grade and I had a vision dream of some of his classmates he was running around with. Dan was trapped in the corner by spiderwebs and his friends were taking our furniture and destroying it. When he got home from school, I told him of the vision dream and suggested he drop his friends as they were headed for trouble. He listened and two weeks later they broke into the school and destroyed things and stole some things. Dan was wanting to be a doctor and didn't want a bad record against him.

Dan was a junior or senior in high school. When this happened, he came home from school and I had been down on my knees praying. I told him what the Lord showed me.

In the vision, I saw his classmates getting ready for a party. They were planning a beer blast party. I saw them all ending up in jail. He came in and I confronted him. He said how did you know about the party. I said the Lord showed me.

I told them I would buy him his friends a six-pack of beer and they could drink it in the parking lot in front of their friends then get out of there and they did. Next day he ran home to tell me they all ended up in jail as God had shown me.

Last episode, Dan: He went to college in Tucson. First year they had people trying to keep the students from their goals. Had a vision of three men and told this to Dan. Once again, he was spared from trouble. God is so good. And he said, "Mom, they've already approached me and they looked like what you saw."

After settling in Fremont, California after taking off for the summer doing God's work, Paul, Dan, Lelia, and I went to Kansas and ministered at my aunt and uncle's church. The minister was teaching any day they were going to be raptured but I told him by teaching them this, they had lost power with God and were sickly. My uncle said it was all true. No love offering from that church at all.

On to Alabama, met a small lady prophetess and her husband. Had good ministry there. Many deliverances. Kept in touch with them for many years. At the moment, their name slips my mind.

Leaving Alabama we went on to visit friends in Colorado and up in the sheep country. Their names were Campbells. Years later we met them again in Phoenix, Arizona.

One experience on this trip, we cannot forget was we ran out of gas out in the country and we stayed to see if we could get a few gallons from the farmer until we could get to town. We asked the farmer and he said no they did not have any. God spoke to me and said that they had lied. He was going to let the tornado take out the farm because they did have some to give. After seeing this vision, the young fellows came out and started pumping gas in our car. God told me He showed them the same vision. I could not help but laugh to myself.

After leaving Colorado, we ended up in Fremont, California. Stayed there for a while, then ended up coming back to Burien, Washington where Diane was born. Paul worked for Boeing. During all this traveling, we were in meetings and saw God do many things.

Before moving to Auburn, Washington, I came from Phoenix and stayed with my sister Trula. The Lord warned me we were going to go through a hard place and trust me it was.

I bought a deep freezer from Kmart and filled it with meat. Also my sister and I canned everything we could get our hands on.

We were going to Portland, Oregon after canning jars. There was a sign alongside the road saying half ton of carrots for $20. So on our way back, we decided to stop and get some. She had a ton truck and of course we did not know what half a ton amount was.

We came into town and canned carrots. Also gave to the whole town. Then my nephew sold sacks of carrots for $40 for rabbit food. Everyone in town called us carrot tops, as both of us had our hair red at the time (lots of laughs)

In three months, we canned 300 quarts of beans, 300 quarts of corn, 200 quarts of blueberries, 200 quarts of apple butter, 300 quarts of applesauce, 100 quarts of beets, 50 or hundred quarts of salmon, 100 quarts of cherry, 100 quarts of peaches, 100 quarts of relish, close to 3000 quarts. This came in handy as we were without work for two years.

One time while we were at the berry field, Tim came running down to tell us a man had scared them upstairs in the bathroom. Paul and I knew the spirits were there but did not know he was teasing the children. Lelia our oldest daughter said to Tim, I'll go up there and prove to you it was nothing. She goes with him and they both come running back and they had heard the same sound. Then I had to let them know we knew there were two poltergeist spirits in the house.

During the five years in the house, many things took place. Our youngest daughter became pregnant at 16 years of age. We had church in our home and were ministers. We stood by her daughter and she gave birth to a beautiful baby girl, Sarah. My daughter and I took turns sleeping on the couch and feeding the baby. We could hear the big man walking up and down the porch, up and down on the porch. I worked and my daughter went to off-campus school and graduated with high honors. At seventeen, she married the father of the child, Mickey Fitzsimmons.

The oldest daughter also became pregnant out of wedlock. She ended up having a baby boy and married the father of the child after graduation, Karey Garmen. During all this going on in our home, Alma McClure, a close friend from Phoenix came and helped us. She was a true blessing to us.

* * *

One year later we came to Spokane to the Schillinger's home and we had a meeting at their home. Fran asked me not to wear as much lipstick as usual as some people there it would offend. I told her I would obey God and we would see.

I went in and sat down across from a lady and her daughter. Of course God said to me to wear my lipstick dark. As I took notice of them, God showed me their hearts. The young daughter had said in her heart, is this the person who's going to speak to us tonight? She was the self-righteous one Fran spoke of.

She noticed God was revealing things to me and asked if I could tell what He was saying. I told her she might not like what God said. She told me to go ahead, so I did.

The Lord let me know that on her job they did not think well of her as she was very self-righteous. Also a girl that worked with her wanted her to go to a Bible study with her but she would not.

As I told her what God showed me and God was not pleased with her. I counseled with her and helped her to change. As a result, she and her mom were one of my intercessors for years as I traveled.

We felt led to invite Mabel to go to the meeting with us. Mabel had been married before and had two daughters. Her ex-husband had been a cruel man and she had lived in Auburn when married.

I encouraged her to move up to Auburn as her youngest daughter was the same age as one of mine. God had spoken to her years before this and told her she would marry again.

We took her to the meeting at the Indian reservation. I found out the man speaking was Don Bradley, the same man who before I married Paul and I was in a meeting in Vancouver, Washington, prayed the prayer of faith for a lady in the wheelchair.

It turned out Mabel gave her heart to the Lord in Don's meeting. God had previously spoke to her the man she would marry his name was Don.

I believe it was love at first sight. She received the Holy Spirit and for the next while they became acquainted at our house.

He decided to buy a home in our area as his first wife passed on to be with God. After a year, they married and he helped her daughter and her baby when it was born. He treated her as a daughter and was so good to her and her mother. The baby used to praise God with him as he praised.

After being in Auburn few years or more, they moved to Orofino, Idaho. He ministered on the Indian reservation where they were deeply loved.

They found out Tina her daughter had a tumor on her head and was dying. She had met a nice guy in Toledo, Washington and was planning on marrying him. He was the son of Lewis Meyers. I knew this family well.

Mabel and Don were planning a trip overseas. He had a vision of two caskets. Then later God showed three. He asked me if God had shown me anything and I said He had not. In

October, they came to see us before they went back to Orofino, Idaho.

At Christmas time, they went and picked up a relative and brought him home for Christmas and took him back home afterward. On their way back home, they hit ice. Went into the river and a truck driver saw it and got chains out and pulled the car out of the water. Don was dead. Mabel was dead. The daughter held the baby over her head and she (Tina) died, and the baby died in the hospital. Tina had planned on giving the baby to my brother John and his wife Marlene when she died of the tumor. God saw fit she went to heaven with her mom and step-dad.

Dreams, Visions & Prophetic Words

Dreams, Visions & Prophetic Words

February 1993

The Feet

One night I had been interceding against the occult. As they seemed to corner me, I would come against them in Jesus' name and through the blood. They would back off and stay a distance from me. After the long length of time, I saw a vision in my dream of two feet. They were only a skeleton of the feet then they took on flesh. Then they began to have toes on the feet. Then I saw them ready to move forward. It was so very important to keep the occult at a distance while the feet were coming together. (End of dream.) Feet ministry getting ready to forward in the earth.

* * *

November 2, 2005

I dreamed I was in a large bed resting with Burel and Katie. Taken from there suddenly, and ended up in my mother's house. She was a night clothes and very beautiful. I had to wear some of her clothes because all I had on was my PJs. Then I wondered how I was to get back to where I came from. I tried the bus, the planes, and decided I had to wait until I was released to go back even as I came.

I was told I was going to take many trips like this and I must get ready to do so. It was like I was in the Brownies like Cub Scouts. As the dream ended, I was getting ready for another journey elsewhere. Katie and Burel are truckers and their bed is on the road driving.

2014 Dream of Colville

There was a large swimming pool and I was with four other women carrying large white blankets walking around pool. We were crying buckets of tears. After going around the pool many times, I went up to the pool and jumped into it. I do not swim but was not afraid to jump.

As I went in, I got into a fetal position and began to intercede. All of a sudden I came up out of the water with a gown on. (It was my glorified body) In back of me was a Rose of Sharon bush. It was so beautiful. All of a sudden I saw myself standing in my regular body observing this sight.

The Lord spoke to me and said, "The Sons of God are getting ready to come to birth." As I looked upon my glorified body, I was made to know there is not a more perfect birth than the water birth. End of vision dream.

Tim's vision 2015: The first part, he said he heard bombs going off in America. The second part: He saw clouds swirling outside the window. He walked to the door and he and his wife looked out and in the heavens was Jesus on a white horse with many crowns on his head. The whole heaven was filled with white horses and riders. End of vision dream.

2016

January. Tim was at work at Boeing in Everett, Washington. He heard the earth begin to shake and knew Seattle had been hit with the big quake. He ran out of the factory as fast as he could and found total devastation outside, trees uprooted etc. End of vision dream.

Tim's 49. At 44 years old, he was in Colorado and saw a vision of a dream I had some fifty years ago. He came by our place on the way home to Seattle began to tell me about it. I said, "Son, I have not told your dad about that one." He said, "Mom, you didn't tell me this one. You know I foresee the future. I'm futuristic."

Glimpse of Zoe's Revelations from 2017

1. Found out I had cancer and had, had it for eleven years. The Lord showed me a vision where He took a rolling pin and pressed the cancer out of my body. At the time, I did not know I had cancer. The next night, I felt His presence on me.

   After finding out I had cancer, I chose not to have my breast removed. They said I had cancer in each breast. I went to see Bruce Allen and his wife. They said stand on what God showed me and I did.

   Before I woke up one morning, Jesus had His hand outstretched with rose petals in His palm. He told me to buy rose petal tea and it would take the cancer out of my body. I've been taking it for over a year. The cancer appears to be gone.

   I asked God to give a preacher on TV a word for me. I always called my cancer a nodule. I asked the Lord to have a preacher say there's a little old lady out there with a nodule on her breast with cancer. She's not too worry as you were going to take it away. (And God did.)

2. Jesus was driving a bus I was on. He took me close to dangerous waters and I was not afraid. I did not seem to be afraid as I knew the driver. God was in charge of the bus. We came to a bump and I asked Him why it was bumpy? He said there was a school of fish we were going over. And I said, "I love to fish for souls." Then we came to shore and up around the big cliff on a high mountain place where He left me off. I knew I would be healed. A great promise. I am now healed.

3. Was on my way to the beauty parlor one Friday morning and God spoke to me, and said, "If I am in you, how can death have any hold on you? No death can be in your body as I, the Lord, am life.

4. Have been studying on the glory of the Lord. Went to foot doctor as my feet were swollen. Found out later it was my blood pressure medicine doing it to my feet. Changed that and no problem since.

   As I came out of the door at clinic where doctor had examined me, a girl followed me out to the car. I rolled down my window and asked if anything was wrong. She began to tell me as I came through the door, my face turned into a ball of light. I was reminded of Jesus when they were to take him in the temple. He turned into light and walked out and they could not see Him (son of light.) Found out what I'd been studying on the glory of the Lord was true. (We are sons of light.)

   2018 added notes: Red book: "1697 Prophecy" by Jane Leade. She said God let her open a seal and she found out the sons of God will be sealed with a ball of light on forehead.

5. Three or so weeks later, I went to Rosauer's grocery store and as I came out of the store a woman came up to me and said, "Lady, you are glowing." I told her it was the Lord that she was seeing. And she agreed, as she was a Christian. We shall be sons of light as Moses came off the mountain his face glowed until they had to put something over his face it was so bright.

6. **(2018)** I believe it was in January, I went to the bathroom about 6 AM and went back to bed. Went into a sound sleep and began to prophesy for over two hours. As I prophesied, I spoke to the Sons of God to come forth. I saw in a vision one of the Sons of God and he lives in Pendleton, Oregon. He's been quite sick. This side or that side, he is a Son. The Lord said, "Sons come forth, as the wind of God is getting ready to blow over America. It will be turbulent at first but will smooth out later."

   2018 The top of the building inside was restored to something that glowed like the lovely Aurora Borealis in Alaska.

* * *

2018

Also had dream of Karen, Dan's wife. We would be close. We have always loved her. She's a good wife and mother to their children. God is faithful and believing Him to reveal Himself to them.

* * *

5.5

Had a vision the rain of the spirit had begun to fall. I hear it is happening in different places. Muslims are getting saved and many other religions also.

God spoke to me one morning and said if God is with Trump who can be against him. (Comment next to this paragraph says good.)

* * *

June 19 – 20 first dreams after Sandra's death

This took place in an airport. Sandra worked for the airlines on technical work and was highly needed. I was visiting her and they had a place there for us to sleep. Her bed was next to mine and we slept with our backs facing each other. She woke up and had to go to work. I was able to stay in bed and rest and dream. Sandra means protector and defender of men.

Sandra also was my Holy Spirit taking care of me while I was in this waiting period before God. Waiting for my instruction and when to leave and what I was to do as I went.

June 22, 2018

I dreamed last night I won the lottery and was getting ready to go collect on it.

July 2018

Had a vision dream of Dave and Alice, pastors of Dream Center and they were taking God's people to a refuge-like place. We all had to leave our homes and flee. People including myself had to leave their homes and go to wherever God told them to go. Our homes were taken over by an antichrist spirit. The only way I got away from them was through the Spirit of God through my finger I pointed at them and many dropped dead trying to take me and they could not. I was able to hold the enemy at bay until everyone got out safe.

At this time, God spoke to me to get off Facebook. It was antichrist. Soros backs up the man who owns Facebook. Soros killed the Jews during the Holocaust and took their property and money. He is out to take America down. God is in charge and I thank him for that.

* * *

September 21, 2018

I had a dream of Dan. He was to meet us at a specific location. We were driving someone else's car and were on our way to meet Dan. We arrived up in the mountains and were stuck there for a while as a big flood hit and covered all the roads we were to take to get to our destination.

Finally the water receded and Paul decided to see if he could go further or come back where we found refuge from the storm. I was shown Paul could not go through to meet with his son. Got a call from Dan and it was flooded from his place to where we were to meet. He was coming from another way and it was flooded also. We were at a lodge. The lodge was a safe spot. End of dream.

* * *

October 2, 2018

Dreamed my husband bought a place without me knowing about it. When I went to see it, it was so dirty and needed cleaning bad. We cleaned it up and my brother Melvin from heaven helped in restoring it to a lovely place. Ceiling showed it was turquoise. As I looked around there was about twelve tables and they all had names of family on them. It was as though we had to feed them. I was wondering how and it appeared there was a crowd and many people were helping to prepare the food.

I appeared to be worried how we were going to do all this. They took the deli down and put in new place to prepare food and serve it to people. I noticed a board with each table's name on it. It represented a whole family

Twelve angels to take them (perfect order) greater mantle. Heavenly knowledge. After remodeling, we opened the doors and let them see in. Liked what they saw. Everything in order. (Old had to go) (perfect order) great place, where I can do a lot.

Note on side of page: Take to new level. Up to heavenly realms of understanding. New way of feeding to them.

We owned the next house and were feeding them out of it. Then when the house was in order, we tore down our house and built a new place for feeding the people.

Colorado

Tim some years ago had a vision of us with prefab houses and red cabins out in front. We were giving people food to eat out of it.

Paul's mother, twenty-five or thirty years ago, had the same vision. I also had it. I'm sure if it's to be, it will be.

Another of Tim's experiences… He and his friends went into a pub to eat dinner. Tim had drifted from God at this time and didn't expect what happened. The girl came to take their orders and all of a sudden God spoke out of him and asked her what she was doing with the gift that was in her.

She was surprised and looked at him funny. She took the orders and when she left God showed him her past, present, and future and he told it all to her. As they got ready to leave, she came to him with tears in her eyes and said, "I thought I had missed God." It shows that God can use even a backslider, if need be, to get us back where we should be.

Romans 11:29 For the gifts and calling of God are without repentance. He came back to the Lord a short time later.

* * *

Tim when he was young he was going to Yakima to help a girl move he knew. I prayed God would give him an angel experience. As he was driving over there, he felt led to pick up a man, which he did not ever do.

When the man got into the car, he immediately began to talk to him about the Lord. He said the man told him things like I would say to him and this took place all the way to Yakima.

Having arrived, he let the man out when he suddenly disappeared from his sight. He had entertained an angel unaware. He was one.

* * *

Had a dream on the wall between Mexico and America. I woke up in the Lord said for me to pray and have the church people pray. That He would send big angels and put them on the wall and people would see them and a revival would break out down there. I am sure praying hard for this.

* * *

A number of months ago I went to Bruce Allen's meetings and he told me I had not asked largely enough. I said you mean $58 million's not enough and he said no. (So I have asked largely.)

After this, God reminded me of Him showing me three lady angels coming and giving me a formula that would keep the highways from decaying. This could bring in much more money. (Infrastructure)

* * *

Dream/vision: October

One day I was in my bedroom and I said to God how long does it take to go to heaven? Immediately I was caught up to heaven where I saw my mother. She looked to be 25 years of age with almost black hair and it was long. She turned around and waved at me and I at her and I was back at my bedroom. One second up, one second back.

Paul's dream (April 2019)

He dreamed he caught the 410 bus and I was not with him. He thought it meant he was going to heaven. He told me he would miss fixing breakfast for me. And I told him, I'd miss it too. The children had decided to give Paul his 90th birthday party and he decided, if he died, why have a party? The bus was 410 and Paul's birthday was 4/15. I told him if he died I would have a nervous breakdown and I would need them all here to help me. Was so glad when it did not come to pass. We just need to know how to interpret our dreams.

May 1, 2019

I had a dream Irene Huffman passed away. Her coffin was pink. I also saw a blue coffin and knew there would be someone close passing soon.

May 6, 2019

On the news, Trump and them sign $2 trillion for infrastructure and highways. Thirty or thirty-five years ago, I was shown three lady angels giving me a formula of a resin to be put on highways and they would not decay. Financial blessing coming our way.

May 8, 2019

On the news, they are saying the polls are getting ready to flip and I saw it back in 1968 or 1969. (Isaiah 24 and 25).

Mary Church in Portland (Sandy)

They were having a rummage sale. This man walked up to them. He needed shoes, clothes, food, etc. They rushed to wait on him and even made sandwiches for him. They invited him to church and told them they would pick him up at a certain place. He was not there. When they arrived at the church, he was there.

They noticed as people greeted him, they would start crying. After the meeting, they asked him, if they could take him to lunch. He agreed and so to lunch they went. They asked what kind of work you did and he replied, "I heal souls." Getting ready to leave, they asked him if they could drop him off somewhere. He said, "I'm where I should be" and vanished before their eyes. We never know when we entertain angels unaware.

Vision at night May 21, 2021

1. A group of us were praising the Lord and the power of God was flowing like a river. It appeared revival had come to us.
2. A group of us were together again this time our voices were taken over by the Holy Spirit and God was singing through us and it was so heavenly.
3. A man came at me like a charging bull and hit me in the stomach and knocked the wind out of me. He circled around again to come at me. I pointed my finger at him and told him to drop dead and he did. I then told his father to go over and pull a sword out of the ground and he would live. His father was moving to the sword to do as I told him to and I woke up. End of vision. (Some people did examine the body and told me he was dead.)

(Our heavenly Father could have been his father that went to pull the sword out of the ground.) And of course he would live by His grace.

Vision dream November 6, 2021

I was at someplace where I needed a ride home. I asked this lady if she could take me home and I would pay her. She was like a babysitter and it was a job. She said yes and she gathered her family together and started to take me home. She said she must drop her family off first.

We drove up this mountain and we were pretty high up. We got out and went over to a cliff and she had us all hold on together and jump off the cliff.

At first I was afraid, but they told me I need not fear and we jumped down. We went to a level where we went to the right and up into their house. It was a humble home and her husband was a teacher of God's Word. Her children, some teens, were very spiritual.

Her husband said he would fix us a bite to eat. He had had an illustration out in a side room about God's gardens. Very unusual.

We fellowshipped on the deep things of God. I showed them I could levitate and up to the ceiling I went. They showed me many spiritual things they had been taught and great fellowship.

Next scene: We had looked out the window and looked down from the height above and it was so beautiful. All of a sudden the house began to move and it went around to the left as the earth moved. You could see they were afraid it was going to crumble.

Then they explained how they needed to move but had no place to go.

Then we decided it was time for a meeting that was planned in the valley. At the meeting, someone gave the man's wife a fur coat and hat. Also the husband received a coat down below his knees. Very nice one and possibly wool.

The meeting was unusual as they dramatized. Her with her fur and hat and he with his coat. The teens were having a meeting around the corner in a room.

Through a word of knowledge and some boxes, they illustrated the scenes. In one box, it said God is not through with the ship yet (America). Other boxes gave many meaningful illustrations. (Spiritual)

All of a sudden, we were drawn to the room of the teenagers and they had a revival going on. (All out revival) I knew I was to help them to go safely and gave them that envelope filled with money. They were blessed.

* * *

Had a dream Dan came, I assumed to Colorado to help move us out of two rooms where we lived. He came to help Tim move us and he was the old Dan I knew years ago. I couldn't help myself and made a fuss over him. Felt great love we had when he was younger.

I was in bed with a lady because I had no place to sleep. She started throwing the covers off and I could not rest there. I'd come there to be taught by this lady but could not rest. So I went downstairs and my brother Marvin was lying and resting in the bed toward the back and Mom was resting in a bed up front. There was a mattress on the floor by her side and I laid down by her and was at rest. Mom's in heaven so is my brother Marvin.

* * *

Had vision I got up one morning and looked in my mouth and I saw the Lord had given me a mouth full of teeth. A miracle!

Karl (wings) were silver. Each wing redemption to millionaires 40 types of gifts.

Melody From

She was a classmate from high school. Melody ended up in the nursing home before she went to heaven. She would curse, scream out until they didn't want her there. Her daughter and I knew another spirit had taken her over. We prayed her body would go home to heaven and be with her real spirit. Two weeks went by and I saw her on the slab and she was smiling. One night she went to sleep and never woke up and a smile was on her face.

Recently I was caught up to heaven in a dream and saw Melody there. She was bored in heaven. She seemed to not have anything to do. So I took her to a leading choir director and enrolled her in the best heavenly choir. She was a good singer, always loved God. Melody found her place as she had a beautiful voice.

Fran Schillinger

First part of dream she had a business in heaven and she was an interior decorator. Second business, she was a seamstress making beautiful glorified dresses. One was teal and chiffon and had a beautiful necklace with it. Second dress was a forest green with sparkles.

Third part she had a plants in the back of businesses. There was a Lily of the Valley and next to it I planted a red rose plant.

I had this dream one day before a friend of mine, Sunny, who had once been a white witch, died the next day. God had saved her at our church thirteen years ago. The red rose plant was her, God showed me. The Lord is the Lily of the Valley.

Dream

Mansion on a hill, small. Quietness away from the world. Went upstairs to master bedroom and there saw Christ and I began to talk to Him. Gave me a couple sentences and pointed toward the closet, the door inside closet, secret door which held a room full of people.

The Lord had made a comment. Then He gave me a blessing before leaving me. I went downstairs to the driveway. Saw a man who offered me a ride to a town where my car was. I said yes. He took me down and he had a blessing to the village square.

"Stop, there's my car."

He did not listen and drove past my car and dropped me off at the store. (Be careful of being manipulated by anointing or fellowship of others/ministers.

Dreams given to Zoe

1. We were in a big building with about 1,000 people. Had music we were trying to get people to worship God. Some were trying, others unconcerned.
2. Finally went outside and Mom and Leota were sitting on the steps. I said to them why don't you come help us with this crowd? I was reminded of the Scripture saying even if they come back from the dead, they would not listen or hear.

(Note on side of page: Mother and sister Leota in heaven.)

Bench in park, chain around ankle, sitting on bench waiting to be released in world but waiting for full release

Standing in some room had black wavy hair cultivated, secured with 12 red roses. I thought it looked pretty good twelve roses for apostolic aristocratic heritage like a castle and thought it was to be changed and started to like it. Redecorated large dome ceiling. Roof outside needed to be replaced.

Bill Purfoy's brother in heaven, younger brother's wife in South Africa

I walked into the building and found myself in heaven. Bill Purfoy came over to me and introduced his younger brother and his wife to me. So I saw what his wife looked like and it was his brother's first wife that had been in the Jim Jones mess and had given her life drinking the poisoned lemonade. At the time writing this, the younger brother is still alive with his second wife. (unusual)

Recently asked the Lord how quick I could go to heaven and back. I was in my bedroom and the Lord caught me up in the spirit and I saw Bill Purfoy, a minister friend I knew in Arkansas, also Phoenix. He and another man were busy doing something for God. I looked over and saw my mother, young and beautiful. I waved at her and she waved at me. God was showing me how easy it is to go to heaven and back. It was two seconds up, and two seconds back.

* * *

Bev Wheeler, a dear friend of mine from church, went home to be with the Lord. She had the inner ear infection and I had been taking her food with others from the church. She'd given me three totes of squares to make children's blankets, when I get to Colorado. Also her sewing machine. One month before her passing, the Lord had shown me He was going to take her home. But I'm still surprised it was so soon. (Lovely soul)

Right now a vision I had thirty-five years ago is coming to pass. I saw Hawaii underwater and the mountain there is blowing high and wide and looks like it's going to be evacuated and go underwater. Sad thing to happen.

Years ago while living in Alameda California, I saw L.A. under a mile of water. That's been over 40 years ago. Thank God for prayers, it has not happened yet.

Before Mount Saint Helens erupted, I saw it a year or two before. In my vision, I saw the trees like matchsticks and that's how it looked after it happened. I saw it missing Toledo, Washington and hitting Castle Rock and it did. Lots of my friends lost their homes on the Toutle River. All as God revealed it to me.

While living in Oakland, I saw the San Franscisco bridge buckle up and go into the ocean. God has us leave Oakland in 1966 after Tim was born. God said He wanted us out of there before the bad things happens. We were there a number of years and we loved the weather.

Prophetic Words

Zoe, I have kept you strong all these years to be a strength to others. I have kept you strong to strengthen my bride and bring healing inside of her. You have seen the torment. You have seen the place of bondage. You have revelation to speak into people. Yeah I have anointed you, Zoe, with words of wisdom and wise is he that wins souls… And I say to you that you have an unlimited wisdom given by my spirit to give others… I will anoint you even to your bones. Your bones I will make strong says the spirit. I will take out anything hindering your bones in your body and strengthen you today. Even a new strength goes in you and upon you says God… And I will break yokes of bondage around you like popcorn. It will just pop, crack, and go off of you… And he says trust me for the supernatural because, girlfriend, I'm a supernatural God, and girlfriend, you and I are of the same loincloth. ~ Kim Sager

Millie Hill

I say to you tonight I'm sending you into places that you always went and you have always proclaimed and you have always done battle. But he says, your weaponry is dull I'm going to send you new weaponry. And you're going to have some cutting edge things happen and you are going to be astounded says God. You are saying, well, my sword got a little dull, but I'm saying to tonight that your sword is going to be piercing the darkness again. The gift of intercession, proclamation, and declaration. More of the glory says God.

Larry

I say to you it is a new day and I say to you that all things are passing away and there is a fire birthed in you by my kingdom that you did not know before says the spirit. And yeah, I have delivered you says the spirit. Larry, God is going to punch holes in the darkness of the fabric of men's souls and you're going to see exploits and signs and wonders. Do not worry about (Somebody's name) as I have my hands upon her and powerful demonic things have happened but I'm going to be giving you a new artillery and a weaponry to take down the power of darkness. Fire, fire, fire of God all the way through.

Gladys Oakley McEwen, Zoe's mother

Gladys Oakley, Zoe's Mother

I, Gladys Oakley, was born in Traverse, Barry County, Missouri, on June 25, 1899. My parents, Melvin and Maude Oakley, owned and operated a country store and ran both the store and post office in Traverse. We lived upstairs over the store.

I have three brothers, Clarence, Kenneth and Oscar. That was our family. It was oil lamps for lights, water carried from a well, and wood for heating and cooking. Later it was coal for heating and kerosene for cooking.

Since my mother was in poor health, and my father was blind, they had to give up the post office. At the age of nine, I began helping in the store. One of the many items carried in the store was patent medicines, so my father became quite an expert on them and was often called "doctor."

He would not put the medicines on the shelves until he had tested them on his family so that he could tell his customers how they worked.

Some of the medicines found on the shelves were Doan's Kidney Pills, Camphor, Turpentine, Rock candy, Black Drought, Dr. Price's Favorite Prescription, Lydia Pinkham's medicine for women, Senna Tea, Epsom Salts, Quinine, Calamine Liniments, Nature's Remedy, Vaseline and Mentholatum.

He also suggested such home remedies as mustard poultices for congestion and bad colds, an onion poultice for fevers, cough and colds, bluing for bee stings, vanilla for burns, skunk oil for colds, goose grease for colds, asafoetida for warding off diseases, cow dung for poultices for blood poisoning, Vicks Vapor Rub for hemorrhoids (discovered by me when I thought I was using Vaseline).

Flour to stop blood in an emergency, kerosene for colds, vinegar and salt to soak out inflammation, catnip tea for baby's colic, raisins to thin the blood in the spring, prunes for constipation, mare's milk for whooping cough, and prayer.

My father was told by three doctors that he would die unless he had a bowel tumor removed by surgery. He refused to have the operation and instead, in keeping with his faith in home remedies, had his Christian friends come and anoint him with oil and pray for him. He died 37 years later.

Special vacations were few and far between during my growing-up years and consisted mainly of summer church camps. I had two in Missouri. I attended my first one when I was eight years old, a camp meeting at Golden, Missouri, located about 20 miles from our home. My Aunt Maddie was a preacher and wanted to attend the camp, so my brother and I made the trip to Golden with my brother driving the team and wagon. It was a rough ride on a rocky road.

We slept in a tent with our bedding on the straw-covered floor, attended meetings in a tent where we sat on rough boards and ate in a tent where our meals were served on tables of rough boards. There were 10 days of services with breakfast at 6:30 a.m., morning service from 8:30 to noon, afternoon service from 2 to 3 p.m., and an evening service after supper.

We played lots of games during our free time in the afternoons. I was bothered with the toothache, but they prayed it away. The meals were great and I enjoyed waiting on tables. We waved tree boughs to keep the flies away from the food. My next vacation happened when I was 15 years old.

My brother and I took our first train to Marshfield, Missouri, about 60 miles away, to spend our Christmas week vacation with our cousins. While there, I enjoyed the horseback riding and my first black minstrel show.

After graduating from the 8th grade, I found I could obtain a third grade teaching certificate by completing the 9th grade passing the exams. This all ended in April 1916, when, due to my mother's illness, we had to sell the store and move to Colorado.

My father obtained a homestead of 320 acres of land north of Hasty, Colorado, while my oldest brother, Clarence, also obtained a homestead of 320 acres of land in the same area. Our family lived in a one-room house on the homestead where they lived six months of the year. My brother Clarence lived in an adobe house on his homestead. You could not obtain a homestead unless you live there at least six months of the year.

Since my mother had to work to help us live, I quit school and went to work for the Rocky Mountain Bell Telephone Co. where I worked until I got married. My brother Kenneth, also worked in town so he and I bought a house, paying for it the same as rent which we lived in while we worked and which our parents could also live in during the six months of winter when they didn't have to live on the homestead. My brother attended school during the winter.

Our family had a great love for animals and they were always an important part of our lives. From time to time we had cats, dogs, horses, cattle, ducks, and goats. We had many dogs, but it was always a tragedy when we lost one to highway traffic.

I married Lee McEwen on April 14th, 1919, at Lamar, Colorado. Lee's parents were William and Lannie McEwen. He was born on December 4, 1894, in Buttle County, Missouri, the third oldest of nine children. Lee moved with his parents to Alfalfa County, Oklahoma, in 1898 to homestead 160 acres in the Cherokee Strip. When Lee was 21, his father brought him and his oldest sister, Nora, to Kiowa County, Colorado, where each acquired a homestead of 160 acres. In 1915, with the coming of World War I, Lee enlisted in the Army. He served 13 months with the 7th Engineers in France and was pensioned off with a disability at $12 per month.

After our marriage, we went to Oklahoma to see his folks. Since Lee was reared as a farmer and rancher, he decided to stay there and farm. When we learned we were expecting our first baby, Lee knew I wanted to be with my mother when the baby was born. He asked me if I wanted to go to Colorado in a covered wagon. Of course I said, "yes" as that meant high class travel.

After 30 days on the road, through snow and helping cars out of ditches, we arrived in Lamar, Colorado the day after Thanksgiving. We tried farming here for three years, but we gave it up, sold out, and moved to Topeka, Kansas. We had three acres there, a nice house, and a beautiful garden. There was only one drawback. The place was located near a rock pit and every time they blasted rock it would cover our place with rock.

We stayed there for one and one-half years and finally sold out to the rock pit operator. We moved back to Lamar, Colorado to farm the combined 640 acre homestead of my folks and brother, where we lived for 10 years.

Lee built an 18 x 20 foot underground or dug-out house with only one partition. He cemented the floor and walls and this kept us warm. The other room served as a cooler. It was pretty crowded for two adults and seven children. It got really crowded one year when there were nineteen living in the house at one time.

This resulted when a blizzard struck and marooned us for 52 hours. It was so bad we could only feed the stock but couldn't milk the cows. The milk dripping from their udders froze, making them very uncomfortable. We started out with a gentle team of horses and had to break the rest for farming. By the time we had enough horses broken, I learned to drive four head of horses attached to a cultivator.

Our farming was all dry land with no irrigation. After a few good crops, we were able to buy an iron horse – a Farmall tractor. Soon we were beset by bad luck. As Lee broke up the sod, Dust Bowl days set in – dust, drought, hail storms, and years of horror!

Most of it was our own fault, but we realized it too late. We raised beans and black-eyed peas, but after the harvest, there were not enough stalks and roots to hold the dirt. We had a herd of dairy cattle here. One of our best milkers had an udder badly damaged in a barbed wire fence. It was so bad we were told to have her butchered.

Lee couldn't do it, but since he had to be gone for three days to find our horses on the range, he told us to get a neighbor to butcher the cow. The children and I did not want to give up on her, so we cried, prayed and treated her. It hurt her so much, we had iron hobble her hind legs and stanchion her to treat her. We bathed her bag with warm milk and bag balm, and used a quill from one of our duck's feathers so that the milk would flow better. She healed up fine and was saved.

Later on, we lost most of our fine stock and prize bull to what the vet called Anthrax, a bowel disorder. One day we cut open a heifer that had just died and found a quart of thistles and sand in the stomach. Nothing would pass. It was a combination of thistles and sand that they were eating that was killing them, not Anthrax.

The thistles were the fastest growing plant that we had and the cattle were attracted to them in the spring. The thistles would blow about and get caught in the barbed wire fences which allowed the blowing sand to catch on them and caused the deadly potion. Losing our stock was more serious than losing our crops.

After ten years and the loss of our crops and animals to hail, dust, and drought, we finally had to give up. In 1935, we moved back to Oklahoma where Lee was raised. It was the same sad story there!

A flood took our first crops and our second planting failed due to no rain. About this time I also had teeth failure. I had lost all my upper teeth except three in front, and I decided I would have them pulled. I answered a mail ad that advertised an upper plate for $5.95. I contacted the local dentist to have my three teeth pulled and one who told me that dentists eat turkey, too. I paid him with two turkeys.

As usual, Lee told me I was crazy, but I ordered the upper plate anyway from the mail order house in Chicago. They came and worked fine for five years until one tooth broke off. It was cheaper to buy another plate rather than have the one tooth replaced. I kept the address of the mail order house that furnished my plate and ordered another in the 1970s. The cost of the plate was now $49, and I had to send my broken plate to them so they could make a new one to match it.

We stayed in Oklahoma for the better part of two years. By this time the McEwen family had grown to eight children - Leota, Kenneth, Gladys, Lana, Melvin John, Marvin & Elzora. We were desperate for a permanent place to settle down.

By providence, a letter came from Lem and Jenny Boss at Castle Rock, who had been our old neighbors in Colorado, telling us about the "Land of Paradise" in Washington. They lived at Sunset Lodge on Old 99, between Castle Rock and Olequa. Old-timers will remember Sunset Lodge as being one of the prettiest spots on Old 99, and still is. It used to be a lodging place and gas station with a house that is still there and still occupied.

The Bosses talked about money growing on bushes, fish dipped by the bucket, fruit ankle-deep, ferns, etc. Lee said this is where we are going!! The worst part about leaving Oklahoma was leaving our beloved spotted pony which we all loved very much. There was much crying over leaving the pony.

Our family landed at Sunset Lodge on July 2, 1936, and soon located on the old Schnurstein place. It was a nice farm with an orchard and garden. I canned at least 1000 jars of vegetables and fruit from the garden and orchard during each year we were there. Lee soon had a job falling and bucking timber. The family soon learned with the Bosses meant by the "Land of Paradise."

Money growing on bushes, blackberries and strawberries – the kids earned money for their school clothes picking berries. Fish dipped by the bucket – smelt. Fruit ankle-deep – fallen apples, etc., on the ground. We bought two sows and 10 pigs to eat the fallen fruit.

Fifty-five years later, we are still living in the Toledo area. Trula, the ninth child, was born in Washington in 1940. We lived in two other houses in the Toledo area before building our own home. In 1938, for $600, we bought 40 acres of land on the Spirit Lake Highway. It was good land with several springs on it.

We built a four-bedroom home on the 40 acres and moved into the house in 1939. It is still occupied by my eldest son, Kenneth. The lumber for the house came from the Hudson Bay Trading Post. Lee and the children and in-laws wrecked the Post, hauled the lumber, and built the house.

In recent years, I gave five acres to each of the girls and two of the other boys and kept five acres for myself. Some of my children sold their five-acre plots of land for more than $5,000 each.

In 1969, Kenny bought a nice modern house for me in town in exchange for my five-acre plot. The house is located across the street from the New Life Assembly Church and serves as a half-way house for my family and friends who attend the church and its activities. I still live in the house and will until my Jesus calls me to His home in heaven.

In the thirties and forties in Washington, we had to create our own entertainment. There was no television, only radio and not too many cars for travel. We had monthly neighborhood parties, birthday parties, picnics with ball games, and plenty to eat, holiday celebrations, and the like. We had wonderful neighbors, and they liked to have fun.

I became interested in physical therapy in 1942. After attending my mother and father's fiftieth wedding anniversary on September 25, 1942, in Lamar, Colorado, I visited my brothers in Oklahoma, Kansas, and Nebraska. I was very tired, and one brother suggested that I had lived in rainy Washington so long that I had moss on my back. He took me to a chiropractic clinic in Wray, Colorado and said I could get rid of the moss there.

The nurse put me in a reclining steam cabinet, and since it was all new to me, I thought I was a goner. Then I showered, and she gave me a Swedish massage. I asked her where she had learned to do this. She said the local doctor had taught her, but she also said that you go to school to learn it or take a mail-order course.

When I got home, I found an ad about massage in a Wild West magazine and sent for information. When my husband saw it, he blew up and said I didn't have the brains or education to do it. I kept receiving literature for several years, but didn't do any more about it until later when things came to a head.

My husband, Lee, drank heavily, and I just couldn't take it anymore. I also did not want to farm anymore. I started divorce proceedings in 1948 and got my final decree in 1949. I could get a small check from the state to help with the dependent children, but I did not want to stay on state aid. I was 49 years of age at the time, and Trula was 9 years old. There is an old saying, "Life begins at 40." For me, "Life began at 50" or thereabouts.

Physical Therapy was to be my life's work for 20 more years. I applied for the mail order massage course, completed it, and received my diploma upon graduation in April of 1949 from the College of Swedish Massage, Chicago, Illinois. It was an eight-month class and I paid $1 down and $3 per month for it.

A cousin in Oregon City found me a free steam cabinet and massage table that got me started. I worked out of my home at first, and also after my retirement. It was a 20-year roller coaster career for me as the work was seasonal - from six to twelve months in length.

I worked at a great many places, some several times, as follows: Saint Martin's Hot Springs at Carson, Washington; Johnnie Johnson's Salon in Portland, Ohanapeosh Hot Springs at Packwood; Dr. Grauer of Longview; and Murietta Hot Springs near Los Angeles, where Trula lived and worked after leaving Toledo.

While in Los Angeles with Trula, I also worked for a little while at Bullock's department store. My longest time for work was Soap Lake where I worked for a chiropractor for one year and then went into business for myself for 10 years.

I was gone from Toledo a lot, but each winter I came back to the old home place in Toledo. Trula lived with relatives while I was away, and while she was still going to school. While at home between seasons, I took care of many people who needed help including Mrs. Barnes, Mrs. Kletsch, Grandma Wallace, Mrs. Parent, Mrs. Jacoby, and Douglas Jones.

I considered Soap Lake to be my retirement place of business since I was now 70 years of age, but I still did some massage work in my home. After retirement, I visited my daughter in Phoenix, Arizona. While there I met an old patient from Soap Lake who took me to the Buckhorn Mineral Wells in Mesa.

The San Francisco Giants were going there to get in shape before spring training at Casa Grande. They needed a therapist for two weeks, so I worked there. Gaylord Perry was one of the Giants. It was great fun. Two years later, I did the same thing again. I have a nice autographed picture from the Giants.

In later years, I traveled a good deal, especially after my family was grown. My physical therapy work also took me to many new places. I have made several trips to Arizona and California and two to Hawaii. In 1976, the 200th anniversary of the USA, I went to Virginia and Washington DC and made special visits to the Civil War battlefields and the soldiers' graves.

In 1976, I also had a great trip to Alaska. There I met people who had graduated from Toledo high school in 1936. We had a great Mother's Day picnic while I was there.

Reunions have been a big part of my vacations. After 50 years, I visited my old home in the Ozark Hills in Missouri. I have tried to attend the Oakley family reunions every year in Nebraska. Every 10 years, the Lee McEwen family side has a reunion in Colorado which we try to attend. Every year we always have our own McEwen family reunions in the Toledo Community Park in Toledo.

What has happened to my ex-husband, Lee, my children and me, and the Oakley family, and where do they now live? Lee McEwen passed away on October 11, 1969 at Grand Junction, Colorado. I still live in Toledo, and three of my sons, Melvin, Kenneth and John, still live in the Toledo area on the Spirit Lake Highway. Marvin lives in Yakima, Lana Eckles passed away four years ago, Gladys Bowen lives in Spokane, Leota Allen lives in Yakima, Elzora Golden lives in Federal Way, and Trula Wasik in Riverside, California.

Four of my children, as well as six grandchildren and six great-grandchildren, graduated from Toledo High School. Three of my children left school to enter the service.

In all, 28 descendants of the Lee and Gladys McEwen family have served or are serving in the armed forces of our country. There are 130 or more descendants (so many I can't keep up with them anymore) of the Lee and Gladys McEwen family. The only living member of my Oakley family, besides myself, is my brother Oscar, aged 86, who now lives in Beenkleman, Nebraska.

I am a devout Christian and an active church member. I would like to share some of my deep feelings with you. I am so thankful I gave my heart to the Lord early in my life. My parents were devout Christians and taught me the value of prayer.

Without prayer, I don't think I could have made it through those years on the Prairies. Being a farmer's wife was very hard. There I was, 40 miles from my home, 18 miles from a doctor, neighbors miles apart, plus sick babies, accidents, blizzard, hail storms, crop failures, etc. I cannot praise my Lord enough.

What I Remember

What I Remember

Kenneth McEwen, Zoe's Brother

I was told by mother that my sister Leota Mae was born January 21, 1920 in Lamar, Colorado after a trip from Cherokee, Oklahoma in a covered wagon. On the way, one morning early, it was frosty and mother was climbing down from the wagon seat, when she slipped and fell on her stomach across the wagon tongue. It could've been bad for my sister but she gave God the credit for keeping her and the baby safe.

I came along March 7, 1921 in Lamar, Colorado. Then in the community of Brandon, Colorado, about 20 miles west of Lamar and 4 miles north of Highway 50, my sister Gladys Irene was born May 31, 1922.

She was born in the community of Brandon which is north of Hastings, Colorado, two miles and one mile west. About Gladys to me, as a brother, she was a little pest. I am that fellow you see just above her picture. I guess I was, too, but I do not want to confess. Life was good even though we did not think so at the time. But as time went by, we learned to love each other as we were taught brothers and sisters were supposed to.

While the next year, 1923 December 24, my sister Lana Maude came into being. Now while all this was taking place I do not know what my father did for a living, whatever it was, we survived. It was after this that we took the trip to Topeka, Kansas 1924 in the fall. We were on a train and my sister Gladys got cut on a broken windowpane. I also remember that my baby sister at that time, Lana, cried quite a lot. I am not sure but I think my father went to Topeka, Kansas to labor in a rock quarry. And the quarry was across the street from where we lived.

After we were there for a while, I remember that men would run east on the road yelling fire in the hole. In a few moments, there would be a rumble, then the men would go back to the quarry, and remove the loose rock. Then rig the quarry for another blast.

I was at an age where I never thought of anything but play. My sisters Leota, Gladys, and I would play outside of the kitchen window and make mud pies.

There was a creek about 50 or 75 feet from the kitchen window. Of course, it wasn't very wide and deep, so our mother and father did not have to worry about us getting drowned.

I remember the time when dad brought home a white face cow so we children could have milk. And the cow being a little wild, got loose, and ran over my uncle Perry. It was a funny sight, my uncle lying on his back and the cow jumping over him. As old as I am, it is still clear in my mind.

While we lived there, one night there was lots of noise. We went outside to see a car going by with a naked woman running up the road ahead of it. As far as I know, we never heard what the problem was but who cares.

There was a boy and girl that lived east of us by the name of Johnson, first names forgotten, but they used to come down to our place and play with us making mud pies.

We lived in Topeka about a year and a half when the man ran up the road yelling fire in the hole. As our habits were, we had gone back to the back room as far as possible from any falling rocks, and as usual the blast. This time a rock the size of a man's head came through our roof and landed on a cot that my baby sister had been laying on right where her head would have been.

Well, that was that. Dad bundled us up and we went back to Lamar, Colorado where Grandpa and Grandma Oakley lived. Mother and we children stayed with them until Dad went out on the Drylands to dig a great hole in the ground and build a house over it calling it a dugout.

I believe it to be the year 1925, in November, we traveled in a Ford touring car out to the dugout. On the way, we came to a hill where dad burned the clutch out and had to back up the hill, was he ever angry.

We got in very late at night and I remember faintly Mother and Dad carrying us in and putting us to bed.

One thing I remember about the trip was the cold ride open touring car being wrapped in lots of blankets being bounced around and we kids making the noise, "Ah! Ah! Ah!" to the bouncing of the car. Sound like fun? It was to us.

December came and we had Christmas! What a Christmas it was! We children hung our stockings on the end of our beds expecting toys but instead received a potato, onion, and corn cobs. What a disappointment until Gladys spotted the red fire wagon under the table loaded with apples, candy, oranges, and I'm sure there was much more but memory evades me at the moment.

Dad's birthday was December 4, 1925, age at that time I think was 29. January came with Leota's birthday the 21st. Then came my birthday March 7, 1926 on which I received a cork gun. And immediately took it outside commenced firing it to which brought a loud response from my dad. I was frightening the horses in the corral. All in all, it was a great time in my life, process of learning. Horses are easily frightened by gunfire.

By September, Leota and I started school, east of where we lived, which was only one half mile away. A few months into the school year, the school we were attending closed and we had to go one mile west and one mile south to what was known as North Gageby. For the next seven years we farmed, raised pigs, cows, horses, chickens, and we also raised goats. This is where we were taught to milk cows, feed, and care for all the animals. In the next seven years, we were milking five cows each morning and night.

I believe it was in the spring when mother and I were going to the spring to get water for our cistern. Mother harnessed the horses, hitched them to the water wagon, and climbed to the wagon seat after putting me up first. She made a sound to get the horses started when she dropped one of the driving lines. At that same moment, a colt of one of the mares got tangled in the tugs and caused the teams to bolt and start running uncontrollably. Mother could only sit and let them run. If she pulled the one line, we would've turned the horses in the fence. Which would have been a disaster possibly killing the horses and us.

Well as it turned out, the teams ran north out the north gate and into the prairie, all the while the first line got wrapped through the left wheel pulling the teams in a tight circle until they came to a stop.

After which, Mother climbed down carrying me with her to the ground. Immediately, I being five and half years old said, "Momma, we almost had a runaway!"

My mother had been crying, which turned into laughter and tears mixed. What an experience!

A neighbor had been driving in the same territory saw the trouble we were in and came to the rescue. Straightening things out, got us back up and running, off to the spring and back home with the water.

This is a fresh in my mind as if it had happened yesterday. Many other trips were made to that spring while we were out on the Drylands. And in the years up and until our leaving in 1934.

In the seven years, lots happened. We would get up at four in the morning, milk the cows. My mother and the girls Leota and Gladys turned the separator to remove the cream from the milk, gather the eggs, clean house, do the dishes, make up the beds, and maybe pump water for the animals until we put up the windmill.

While they did all those things, Dad would harness four horses for the plow and four to put on the disc. My job was to take the other four horses on the disc and go over the ground that he had already plowed.

One thing that Dad always told me, "Son, if the horses get spooked, just fall off the seat and head for the nearest fence. Because I can replace the horses but I cannot replace you."

Our hours were daylight to dark, then milk, separate the mike, eat our supper, and go to bed. This took place day after day until the crops were in. While the crops grew, the grind went on until it was time for weed pulling and hoeing to be done. Out of all the work we did, I believe I hated those jobs the most.

I'm not sure but I think 1928 was the year Dad bought the tractor and we had a good crop of corn. The year 1929 came and so did my brother Marvin on October 21.

Our crops were fantastic. 14,000 bushels of corn and I'm guessing three to maybe 4000 pounds of beans. I should remember because my bed was on the floor behind the stove and by harvest ending, my bed was as high as the stove or higher. Things went very well until the market went back in 1929 when Dad took our shelled corn to market, the first load of 65 bushels sold for $0.65 a bushel. The next sold at $0.25 which meant we did not get the bills paid.

I believe we planted another crop and the drought came. Crops dried up, the wind blew, sand covered our fences, and we could not borrow more money to plant again. So Dad did the best thing he could do. He sold off about 80 head of cows, 50 to 60 head of hogs. All of the chickens. The count I do not remember. All the farm machinery, some of the horses. The rest we took to Oklahoma where he sold them and bought another tractor, put in some wheat which washed out when the Madsen River flooded. We lost again.

We had neighbors in Colorado by the name of Boss. My mother kept in touch through letters and they had moved to the state of Washington kept telling us how money grew on trees. After the loss of the wheat crop, Dad and Mother thought that after all, we should take the trip and find out for ourselves.

So my dad put me on the tractor, sent me to the sandhills to hook onto another tractor and combine to harvest wheat. Things went well. Dad took my wages, his wages, the money for the tractor, bought a ton and a half truck. Loaded the family and all our belongings and headed for the state of Washington. We arrived here July 6 of 1936. As told money did grow on trees, bushes, and vines, on the trees were moss, cherries, and apples. On bushes, blackberries, large and small, ferns, on the ground strawberries, on the vines, hops and peas. All I can think of at the moment. But that summer, we children went to work and earned enough for our school clothes. Sure helped Mother and Dad financially.

School year of 1936 my freshman year, just like other years except I felt a little more important. I'm in high school now. Life in school for me was a struggle. No matter how hard I tried, I could not get above a C or B average. Dad always said he didn't expect me to be a genius but he wanted to do my best. Made it through 12th grade and graduated. I was not ready for life in the workforce. There wasn't much work around Toledo, so I went to Seattle with my brother-in-law and found work at Nettleton Lumber company from 1940 to August 19, 1942 when I got the draft notice and decided it would be best to enlist instead.

I enlisted at Fort Lewis and was sent to Sheppard Field, Texas for Air Force training near Dallas-Fort Worth. Nineteen weeks there and then on to Fort Myers, Florida where I took gunnery training air to air firing from a plane. It was very exciting, if you like standing on your head while firing a thirty caliber machine gun while hanging from a strap holding you to the floor of the cockpit.

At 90, I do not think I could do it now. I went from there on to Avon Park bombing range for three weeks of extensive training in the B-26 barn. We were taking our physical to go overseas when the doctor found fungi in my ears. It was the hospital for me and my crew went without me.

* * *

Note: These are short verses written by Ken. Along with special notes written in Ken's handwriting beside the original poems, which are included as well.

To Tim.

Tim, if you are ever far away and feel all alone.
You can look back and think of Mom and home.
When you are cold, hungry, and feel like a stone.
You can look back to that bed, food, Mom, and home.
I tell you this because I've been down the road of life.
When you face the cold hard facts, they cut like a knife.
Remember I, too, thought of bed, food, Mom, and home
and I, at age 88, think of my mom and home.
This young man is special not only in computers but thoughtful in morals.

For Tyson.

Your mom has been a real friend to you.
But you treat her as trash or like an old shoe.
Maybe you should be nicer to her and show love.
Respect her and maybe you will receive from above.
God showed me what a jerk I was before I knew Him.
Believe God and study His word maybe He will then.
Show you where you are wrong and show a way.
To be helpful to your mother and dad they will say.
Thank you, son, God and the Savior richly bless you.
When you study the Bible, follow the instructions, too.
My nephew. The last two I wrote. Kenny McEwen

Reminiscing (It Came to Me)

Once I was able to hang from the rafters.
I stand wondering what I'm here after.
Is it because I'm near the end?
Or will God help me mend?
No matter the trouble be.
Only God can really help me.

Just sitting looking out the window. The title was changed to "It Came to Me" written in Ken's handwriting.

A Feeling

Now that I'm getting old, I feel like cheese with mold.
But isn't it thrilling out of mold, they make penicillin.

Second I wrote. Not feeling good one day.

Brag or Complain

I remember when I wasn't bad to look at.
Now I'm old and just a little fat.
It doesn't really matter what size.
I just hate the bags under my eyes.
Once I had fine wavy hair.
It's like heaven no parting there.
If heaven's the place you'd like to go.
Give your heart to Jesus, He will make it so.
Repent, admit to Him you are a sinner.
He will take you to God, you will be a winner.

Looking in a mirror one day.

My Wife and I

I'm always thinking of my wife.
She has been great in my life.
There are things she'd like me to forget.
She doesn't know how to erase them yet.
Is it the post office or the peanut trees?
Maybe the foothills or the bird at lemon tree.
The cute little things she is always saying.
Keeps the laughter in my heart singing.
Thinking about the cute things Betty says and does.

Things I Cannot Do

As I sit here with my memories rolling.
Trying to remember the things I used to do.
My body wakes me up screaming.
You cannot do the things you used to do.
First I ever wrote.

I Tried

I tried three times to get off my seat.
My brain couldn't remember my feet.
I began to shuffle, my body screamed in alarm.
The muscles I had above are now below my arms.
Third I wrote.

TO THE LIFE OF ONE CALLED AND CHOSEN

Think About It

How does a pill know when it is in the stomach which way to go?
Will it know if it is for the heart, the kidney, the knee, or maybe the toe?
It is amazing to me how the doctor knows if it will do good or bad.
According to the maker of the pill, it might give you something you never had.
Doctors ask what your problem is you tell them what you think, of course.
They go ahead and prescribe something for you that could even kill a horse.
Why can't they be like a veterinary feel, look, and maybe a CT scan or x-ray.
Instead they ask lots of questions you cannot answer, prescribe a pill, and say
"Come back in two or three weeks not knowing that you could die of the effect."
Yes, you are back in two or three weeks and they look at you as you expect.
They find after all their thinking they still haven't cured your ills.
They muse, ponder, yep, that's right, they prescribe another "pill."
Coming back from Doctor's office.

Betty

She is always talking about how great my family was.
My family would hear she was coming and be in a buzz.
She was always happy, bubbling, and a perfect delight.
They would always accept her morning, noon, or night.
Ivan and Gladys would always laugh with glee.
When I thought of Betty and the peanut trees.
Mother and Patty would be very cautious.
When mentioning Betty and the post office.
New York City with all their confetti.
Cannot compare with charming Betty.
About Betty and the fun things with my family.

The Girl I Married

Betty the girl I married 65 years, my burdens she carried.

No matter the trouble I was in, she stayed through thick and thin.

We never reached fortune or fame but we were not to blame.

God had a plan for us to see, He forgave our sins and set us free

To do His will and teach others, boys to be fathers, girls to be mothers.

She was always there beside me never worrying about what might be.

We have laughed and shed tears through our sixty-five years.

We are glad God tarried so we could be together, me and the girl I married.

About how good she has been to me throughout the years.

The Year 1943

The year was nineteen forty three at a Halloween party I met my wife to be.

At the time, she was seventeen but eighteen very soon she would be.

And from a family of thirteen, they were all very wonderful and kind.

A better or more wonderful family of people, you can never ever find.

Many years our relationship grew every year, there was something new.

All troubles and heartaches shared by all were definitely very few.

Our life together will be sixty-five years on February 14 of 09.

Amazing to me how all things that are good can happen to us over time.

Thinking of how I met Betty.

I am Glad

My body is old and does not want to work but the mind is alive and will not shirk.

The body will return to the earth but my spirit will return to God who gave me birth.

After all my work on earth is finished or done, I'll know that the race that I have run.

Was not accomplished for me or by me but Christ who died on the cross to set me free.

My hope for me and my wife, we will be a blessing to God and Christ the rest of our life.

Just feeling down.

God's Grace is Enough

I have walked on the earth and under the sun. Life wasn't great until God made my wife and me one.

I should have been gentle, loving, and kind but instead I was very loud and spoke my mind.

My voice to her was like loud thunder that's not all, I was always making lots of blunders.

It never seemed to bother her at all, she was always there at my every beck and call.

She should have been in tears but she just seemed to love me more through the years.

I'll never be able to undo the hurt she should feel but she never lets it bother; her love is real.

We never talked or thought much about God until that special day He gave us the nod.

It was in a small place, called South Bend. I let God take over and our lives began to mend.

He made me to know our problems were me. On the other hand, she was more like Jesus you see.

We do not worry about the world and all the bad stuff because God's grace is enough.

About my wife and our life.

My Hope

I sit with my mind working trying to comprehend all I've read in God's book.

I realize that no matter how I try, my small brain can never attain for what I look.

Until I come to a greater understanding of God's book, I cannot know His love.

Yet I keep searching for that perfect understanding that will come from above.

I often ask God if I am to have the mind of Christ, why do I keep making mistakes?

Some day I hope to attain the knowledge before to His mansions me He takes.

If by chance, I do not make the goal of this so great a race.

I hope and pray that I will make it by His mercy and His grace.

After Bible study at home.

An Amazing Moment

Midnight. when yesterday and tomorrow meet,

Yesterday backs up 24 hours to become day before yesterday.

And let today become yesterday.

Tomorrow jumps 24 hours ahead to let today take over.

This all takes place in a moment.

At a little after midnight this came to me.

Clean Up

I cook a meal but that is no big deal.
I dirty dish and cup and Betty cleans up.
I make lunch of good things to munch.
I dirty spoon, fork, and such. Betty cleans up.
There is no end, I make a mess. Betty cleans up.
This is not all Betty likes to polish and clean up.
If only she can clean up my life, Betty, my wife.

Poems

Poems have been written for many years.
Some are so sad they can bring you to tears.
Some are so good they will bring you to laughter.
But they can never do as much good as our Master.
He, Jesus, came to set you, me, and all captives free.
He did this by taking your place and mine on a tree.
God loved us so much that He gave us His son.
So that we all His children might all be as one.
In Christ Jesus.

The Trip of a Pill

If you want to get a thrill, just trace the trip of a pill.
It goes in and way down looking for a virus to be found.
What it is looking for you see, is very amazing to me.
Research said it is to do this. How will it know if it missed?
But if it did something good, will it know that it should?
Will it know the virus is detected and someone be affected?
Maybe it will be worse than before giving bad things by the score.
According to the PDR book, everyone should take a good look.
And heed the warning or you could be very dead in the morning.
People are trusting souls, some winding up in deep holes.
All because of the trip of a PILL.

The Pill

Some are pink, yellow, and maybe even brown.
One thing about them, they must go down.
Doctors give them, red, blue, and some white.
To be taken as directed, morning, noon, or night.
They come in all shapes, colors, and size.
When you take them, you wonder if it is wise.
But we take them because the doctor went to school.
And we are hoping and thinking they are not fools.
On the other hand, we know that they are educated.
Then we pray that they are very, very dedicated.
We wait to see if the little fellow would do his thing.
Take away the dizziness, nausea, and the pain.
There again we wait and see if the little guy the pill,
will do what he should do then we pay the bill.

Why Is It?

Doctors that are educated and smart, ask the patient where to start.
They have the tools to keep them from acting like fools.
For some unknown reason, they are not using them this season.
The thing that isn't funny, mostly they're thinking of the money.
For a car or maybe a new boat, shoes, suit, could be a new coat.
Hope I'm wrong thinking it is for self their head at home on a shelf.
The patients are being neglected, the doctors are being disconnected.
From reality, caring and hope with which everyone is trying to cope.
I'm old and not that bad. For the ones that need the help, I feel very sad.
After a trip to Betty's doctor.

Kenny & Family

Tim & wife Cheryl

The McEwen Family News

Fall 1995 (The Voice of 2472 Scottish, Irish American McEwen Households)

Gladys McEwen & daughter-in-law Betty McEwen
Gladys was born June 25,1899 near Flat Creek, MO.
Married Lee McEwen in 1918 and had nine children,
four boys and five girls. Mrs. McEwen lives in
Toledo, WA.

McEwen: The son of Eoghan (well-born).

Gladys McEwen & Betty McEwen

Kenny McEwen & Betty
(Gladys son)

Alberta Johnson

Alberta Johnson

Alberta's father, Charles Johnson, was from Sweden.

Her mother was a Clemens. Samuel Clemens (Mark Twain) was her relative.

There was a movie about the ship they came on to America in 1906 or 1908. (This is your land, this is my land.)

Zoe Golden met Alberta in 1966 or 1967. Alberta had cancer. We prayed for her and God healed her. We became friends and then she was like a part of our family. We went to church meetings together. She wrote down all about them.

Alberta was a retired schoolteacher. She helped my two daughters become good scholars. My oldest daughter became a medical secretary. And my youngest daughter became a nurse and a captain in the Air Force reserves. Alberta taught them how to really study.

My oldest daughter ended up having large daycare centers for children. She made more doing this than being a medical secretary.

We, the Goldens, lived in the house she owned on Indian School road near Scottsdale, Arizona. I worked at a bank there. The house was very close to work.

Alberta owned a trailer in the mobile home court near us in her house. We had meetings in the big den of the house (100 people.) Many souls were saved there. One man, a stranger came one night and I, Zoe, gave a message in tongues. Then I told a group of 100, it did not need to be interpreted because whoever was there got the message. A man came up after the meeting and asked if I knew what I had spoken. I said I didn't. He then told me I spoke in perfect Aramaic. He had been studying in a foreign country the language. He got saved. The message spoke to him. He left a believer. Praise God!

In Alberta's house, I became ill and had strep throat. Three days later, I was delirious and each day I visited heaven. The first day I met people that I had confirmation with about God's word.

The second day, I visited my father and we were on a carpet green grass lawn. We visited all day.

The third day, Alberta's mother, who looked 25 years old, came across the lawn and hooked her arm in with mine and we knew each other. I had only seen her as a 94-year-old in a picture, but I knew her there and she knew me.

As we talked, she came into my bedroom where I was sick and prayed for me and God healed me. I got out of bed as though I had never been ill. I woke up and saw her walk back out through the wall in a blue mist. I cried and went in the living room and was in a rocking chair that her mother had owned. I was totally healed. She came back in the house and put her hand on my shoulder and asked if I was okay, I said, "Yes."

The next day Alberta brought a picture album of her mother and I picked out her picture. She was 25 years old in it.

Alberta cried. She said, "Why doesn't Mom come see me?"

Her mother while on earth healed many people of their afflictions.

Alberta and the Goldens shared many friends together. The Bells came to our meeting. The Huffmans, Sandra and Irene, sometimes her husband. In 1973, we left Phoenix and moved to Auburn, Washington. One or two years later, Alberta followed us. She brought her trailer and put it in a park there in Auburn, Washington. She lived there until she died.

Alberta made many friends and went to Women's Aglow. Also to Christian Men's Fellowship meetings in Auburn. She and Grace Hooper were friends for over 10 to 15 years.

Her friends would go see her in the rest homes she was in, which were many, before she went home to be with Jesus.

Seven years before she passed, Alberta had a stroke. I was at work and the doctor said her vital signs were shutting down and she would be dead by the time I got to the hospital. Paul worked as maintenance at the hospital. And in the afternoon that day, Alberta had a holy visitation by God. The Lord Jesus came and angels touched her and healed her. She was the talk of the hospital for weeks to come. She lived seven or eight years beyond this experience.

When our grandchildren came to see us, and Alberta was there, they loved her dearly. Our grandson Jeremy asked her if he could see her deformed hands. She said, "Yes." Jeremy took her hands in his little hands and touched them all over. Then he picked them up and kissed them. Alberta thought it was great.

Because of her stroke, Alberta was in many rest homes, where three or four people lived. We always visited her and all her friends were faithful. We took care of her for 10 years. I, Zoe, took her out of the last nursing home and was putting her in a home she had been in before and they loved her dearly. And gave her a perm.

The next day we rushed her to the hospital and God took her home. I was so shocked when I saw her in her casket. I realized that she did not have her glasses on. Also forgot teeth and a mortuary fixed her up beautiful.

Alberta was buried in the Auburn Cemetery on a hill overlooking the valley. She would have loved it. Alberta's in heaven and I'm sure God has her working or enjoying Him.

Much love, the Goldens.

McEwen Family Genealogy

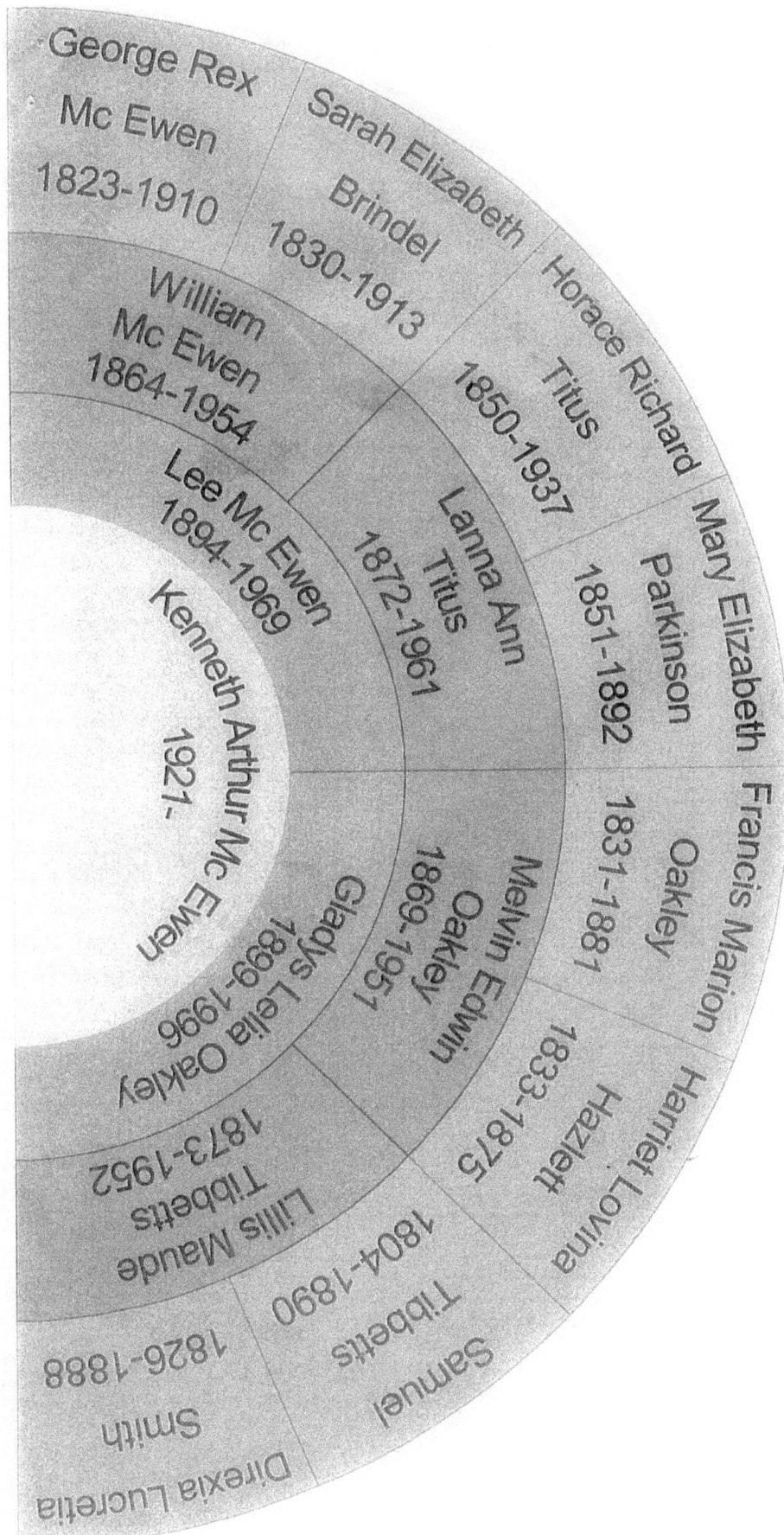

George Rex
Mc Ewen
1823-1910

Sarah Elizabeth
Brindel
1830-1913

William
Mc Ewen
1864-1954

Horace Richard
Titus
1850-1937

Mary Elizabeth
Parkinson
1851-1892

Lee Mc Ewen
1894-1969

Lanna Ann
Titus
1872-1961

Francis Marion
Oakley
1831-1881

Kenneth Arthur Mc Ewen
1921-

Melvin Edwin
Oakley
1869-1951

Harriet Lovina
Hazlett
1833-1875

Gladys Lelia Oakley
1899-1996

Samuel
Tibbetts
1804-1890

Lillis Maude
Tibbetts
1873-1952

Direxia Lucretia
Smith
1826-1888

Family Group Record

George Rex Mc Ewen / Sarah Elizabeth Brindel
C:\My Documents\LEE & GLADYS MCEWEN.PAF

5 Jan 2010   1 of 3

Husband's Name			
George Rex Mc Ewen			
Born	2 Jun 1823	Place Glasgow, Scotland	
Chr.			
Mar.		Place Carlton, Lenrich County, Ontario, Canada	
Died	10 May 1910	Place Republic County, Kansas, USA	
Bur.		Place Washington Cem., Republis, Kansas, USA	
Father		Mother	Parent Link
Husband's other wives			

Wife's Name			
Sarah Elizabeth Brindel			
Born	1830	Place Dublin, Ireland	
Chr.			
Died	18 Nov 1913	Place Republic County, Kansas, USA	
Bur.		Place Washington Cem., Kansas	
Father Lord John Brindel		Mother Lady Mc Mahan *I = SABell*	Parent Link Biological
Wife's other husbands			

Children

1. Sex	Name		
F	Isabella Mc Ewen		
	Born		
	Chr.		
	Mar.	Place	
	Died		
	Bur.		Parent Link Biological
	Spouse Ed Cronan	There are other marriage(s)	

2. Sex	Name		
F	Sarah Elizabeth Mc Ewen		
	Born		
	Chr.		
	Mar.	Place	
	Died		
	Bur.		Parent Link Biological
	Spouse John Edward Parker		

3. Sex	Name		
M	John Mc Ewen		
	Born 18 Dec 1851	Place Carlton, Lenrich County, Ontario, Canada	
	Chr.		
	Mar.	Place	
	Died 1940	Place Republic County, Kansas, USA	
	Bur.		Parent Link Biological
	Spouse Mary Etta Rowley		

4. Sex	Name		
F	Margaret Mc Ewen		
	Born		
	Chr.		
	Mar.	Place	
	Died		
	Bur.		Parent Link Biological
	Spouse Jessie Beers		

5. Sex	Name		
M	George Mc Ewen *made cigars*		
	Born		
	Chr.		
	Mar.		
	Died		
	Bur.		Parent Link Biological
	Spouse		

☒ Check here if other children are listed on additional pages.

Family Group Record

George Rex Mc Ewen / Sarah Elizabeth Brindel
C:\My Documents\LEE & GLADYS MCEWEN.PAF

5 Jan 2010   2 of 3

Husband	George Rex Mc Ewen	Yr. of Birth 1823
Wife	Sarah Elizabeth Brindel	Yr. of Birth 1830

Children (continued)

6. Sex F — Name Agnes Mc Ewen

Born		
Chr.		
Mar.	Place	
Died		
Bur.		Parent Link Biological
Spouse Alexander Cole		

7. Sex M — Name Tom Mc Ewen

Born		
Chr.		
Mar.	Place	
Died 15 Sep 1930	Place Wichita Falls, Texas, USA	
Bur.		Parent Link Biological
Spouse Millie (Quick) Matalock		

8. Sex M — Name William Mc Ewen *Grandfather of Elzora A*

Born Mar 1864	Place Darlington, Langlade, Wisconsin, USA	
Chr.		
Mar. 28 Jun 1886	Place Mankate, Kansas, USA	
Died 14 Apr 1954	Place Cherokee, Alfalfa, Oklahoma, USA	
Bur.		Parent Link Biological
Spouse Lanna Ann Titus		

9. Sex F — Name Mary Mc Ewen

Born		
Chr.		
Mar.		
Died		
Bur.		Parent Link Biological
Spouse		

10. Sex F — Name Janetta Mc Ewen

Born		
Chr.		
Mar.		
Died		
Bur.		Parent Link Biological
Spouse		

11. Sex M — Name James Mc Ewen

Born		
Chr.		
Mar.		
Died		
Bur.		Parent Link Biological
Spouse		

12. Sex M — Name Henry Mc Ewen

Born		
Chr.		
Mar.		
Died		
Bur.		Parent Link Biological
Spouse		

Child 1	Isabella Mc Ewen
Other Marriages:	
George Comer	
Place	
Andrew Minard	
Place	

Family Group Record

Husband's Name: William Mc Ewen

Born	Mar 1864	Place Darlington,Langlade,Wisconsin,USA
Chr.		
Mar.	28 Jun 1886	Place Mankate,Kansas,USA
Died	14 Apr 1954	Place Cherokee,Alfalfa,Oklahoma,USA
Bur.		

Father George Rex Mc Ewen   Mother Sarah Elizabeth Brindel   Parent Link Biological

Husband's other wives

Wife's Name: Lanna Ann Titus

Born	30 May 1872	Place Illinois
Chr.		
Died	8 Jul 1961	Place Cherokee,Alfalfa,Oklahoma,USA
Bur.		

Father Horace Richard Titus   Mother Mary Elizabeth Parkinson   Parent Link Biological

Wife's other husbands

Children

1. Sex M — Perry Mc Ewen

Born	Oct 1890	Place Kansas
Chr.		
Mar.		
Died		
Bur.		Parent Link Biological
Spouse		

2. Sex F — Nora Mc Ewen

Born	Sep 1892	Place Kansas
Chr.		
Mar.		
Died		
Bur.		Parent Link Biological
Spouse		

3. Sex M — Lee Mc Ewen

Born	4 Dec 1894	Place Bates County,Missouri,USA
Chr.		
Mar.		Place
Died	Oct 1969	Place Grand Junction,Mesa,Colorado,USA
Bur.		Parent Link Biological
Spouse	Gladys Lelia Oakley	

4. Sex F — Stella Mc Ewen

Born	Nov 1896	Place Kansas
Chr.		
Mar.		
Died		
Bur.		Parent Link Biological
Spouse		

5. Sex F — Elsie Mc Ewen

Born	Jul 1898	Place Nebraska
Chr.		
Mar.		
Died		
Bur.		Parent Link Biological
Spouse		

[X] Check here if other children are listed on additional pages.

Family Group Record

William Mc Ewen / Lanna Ann Titus
C:\My Documents\LEE & GLADYS MCEWEN.PAF

Husband	William Mc Ewen	Yr. of Birth 1864
Wife	Lanna Ann Titus	Yr. of Birth 1872

Children (continued)

6. Sex	Name		
M	Teddie Mc Ewen		
	Born	abt 1902	Place Oklahoma
	Chr.		
	Mar.		
	Died		
	Bur.		Parent Link Biological
	Spouse		

7. Sex	Name		
F	Pearl Mc Ewen		
	Born	abt 1904	Place Oklahoma
	Chr.		
	Mar.		
	Died		
	Bur.		Parent Link Biological
	Spouse		

8. Sex	Name		
M	William "Willie" Mc Ewen		
	Born	abt 1906	Place Oklahoma
	Chr.		
	Mar.		
	Died		
	Bur.		Parent Link Biological
	Spouse		

9. Sex	Name		
F	Lena or Lana Mc Ewen		
	Born	abt 1908	Place Oklahoma
	Chr.		
	Mar.		
	Died		
	Bur.		Parent Link Biological
	Spouse		

10. Sex	Name		
	Born		
	Chr.		
	Mar.		
	Died		
	Bur.		
	Spouse		

11. Sex	Name		
	Born		
	Chr.		
	Mar.		
	Died		
	Bur.		
	Spouse		

12. Sex	Name		
	Born		
	Chr.		
	Mar.		
	Died		
	Bur.		
	Spouse		

Child 3	Lee Mc Ewen

Notes for Lee Mc Ewen:

Lee and Gladys McEwen were living in Bent County, Colorado in 1930. The census was taken on April 3, 1930 in Precinct 3, Gagely. Lee was a Farmer on a General Farm, living on a rented farm. They did have a "Radio Set."

Lee was registered on a World War I Registration Card. He was living in Lamar, Prowers County, Colorado, was a single man with no dependants. His physical description was given, He was Tall, Slender, with Brown Hair and Brown Eyes, not bald, and no physical disabilities.

While living in Bent County, Colorado where several of the children were born, the eldest son, Kenneth remembers the excitement when the Doctor came to help the Midwife deliver the children. They saw the airplane fly in over the prarie and saw it land, and saw it take off when the Doctor left to return to Las Animas, Colorado. How exciting that must have been!

Husband's Name
Lee Mc Ewen

Born	4 Dec 1894	Place Bates County, Missouri, USA
Chr.		
Mar.		Place
Died	Oct 1969	Place Grand Junction, Mesa, Colorado, USA
Bur.		

Father William Mc Ewen   Mother Lanna Ann Titus   Parent Link Biological

Husband's other wives

Wife's Name
Gladys Lelia Oakley

Born	25 Jun 1899	Place Missouri
Chr.		
Died	4 Jun 1996	Place Centralia, Lewis, Washington, USA
Bur.		

Father Melvin Edwin Oakley   Mother Lillis Maude Tibbetts   Parent Link Biological

Wife's other husbands

Children

1. Sex F Name **Leota Mae Mc Ewen**
   Born 21 Jan 1920 Place Lamar, Prowers, Colorado, USA
   Died 9 Feb 1986 Place Corning, Tehama, California, USA
   Parent Link Biological

2. Sex M Name **Kenneth Arthur Mc Ewen**
   Born 7 Mar 1921 Place Lamar, Prowers, Colorado, USA
   Parent Link Biological

3. Sex F Name **Gladys Irene Mc Ewen**
   Born 31 May 1922 Place Brandon, Kiowa, Colorado, USA
   Parent Link Biological

4. Sex F Name **Lana Maude Mc Ewen**
   Born 24 Dec 1923 Place Out From: Las Animas, Bent, Colorado, USA
   Died 17 Aug 1985 Place Lewis County, Washington, USA
   Parent Link Biological

5. Sex F Name **Melvin Henry Mc Ewen**
   Born 30 May 1925 Place Out From: Las Animas, Bent, Colorado, USA
   Parent Link Biological

X Check here if other children are listed on additional pages.

Family Group Record

Lee Mc Ewen / Gladys Lelia Oakley
C:\My Documents\LEE & GLADYS MCEWEN.PAF

5 Jan 2010   2 of 3

		Yr. of Birth 1894
Husband	Lee Mc Ewen	
Wife	Gladys Lelia Oakley	Yr. of Birth 1899

Children (continued)

6. Sex	Name	
M	Marvin Lee Mc Ewen	
	Born 21 Oct 1929	Place Out From: Las Animas, Bent, Colorado, USA
	Chr.	
	Mar.	
	Died 15 Dec 2008	Place Yakima, Yakima, Washington, USA
	Bur.	Parent Link Biological
	Spouse	

7. Sex	Name	
F	Elzora Jane Mc Ewen	
	Born 11 Jan 1932	Place Out From: Las Animas, Bent, Colorado, USA
	Chr.	
	Mar.	
	Died	
	Bur.	Parent Link Biological
	Spouse	

8. Sex	Name	
M	John William Mc Ewen	
	Born 2 Jan 1936	Place Burlington, Alfalfa, Oklahoma, USA
	Chr.	
	Mar.	
	Died	
	Bur.	Parent Link Biological
	Spouse	

9. Sex	Name	
F	Trula Gale Mc Ewen	
	Born 3 Feb 1940	Place Toledo, Lewis, Washington, USA
	Chr.	
	Mar.	
	Died	
	Bur.	Parent Link Biological
	Spouse	

10. Sex	Name	
	Born	
	Chr.	
	Mar.	
	Died	
	Bur.	
	Spouse	

11. Sex	Name	
	Born	
	Chr.	
	Mar.	
	Died	
	Bur.	
	Spouse	

12. Sex	Name	
	Born	
	Chr.	
	Mar.	
	Died	
	Bur.	
	Spouse	

Husband	Lee Mc Ewen

Notes for Lee Mc Ewen:

Lee and Gladys McEwen were living in Bent County, Colorado in 1930. The census was taken on April 3, 1930 in Precinct 3, Gagely. Lee was a Farmer on a General Farm, living on a rented farm. They did have a "Radio Set."

Family Group Record   Lee Mc Ewen / Gladys Leila Oakley   5 Jan 2010   3 of 3
C:\My Documents\LEE & GLADYS MCEWEN.PAF

Lee was registered on a World War I Registration Card. He was living in Lamar, Prowers County, Colorado, was a single man with no dependants. His physical description was given, He was Tall, Slender, with Brown Hair and Brown Eyes, not bald, and no physical disabilities.

While living in Bent County, Colorado where several of the children were born, the eldest son, Kenneth remembers the excitement when the Doctor came to help the Midwife deliver the children. They saw the airplane fly in over the prarie and saw it land, and saw it take off when the Doctor left to return to Las Animas, Colorado. How exciting that must have been!

Family Group Record

Melvin Edwin Oakley / Lillis Maude Tibbetts
C:\My Documents\LEE & GLADYS MCEWEN.PAF

5 Jan 2010 — 1 of 1

Husband's Name: Melvin Edwin Oakley

Born	4 Oct 1869	Place Toledo,Cumberland,Illinois,USA
Chr.		
Mar.	25 Sep 1892	Place
Died	11 Jan 1951	Place Benkelman,Dundy,Nebraska,USA
Bur.		

Father: Francis Marion Oakley — Mother: Harriet Lovina Hazlett — Parent Link Biological

Husband's other wives

Wife's Name: Lillis Maude Tibbetts

Born	23 Jul 1873	Place Pleasant Grove,Iowa,USA
Chr.		
Died	1 Apr 1952	Place Lamar,Prowers,Colorado
Bur.		

Father: Samuel Tibbetts — Mother: Direxia Lucretia Smith — Parent Link Biological

Wife's other husbands

Children

1. Sex M — Clarence L. Oakley
Born Nov 1892 Place Iowa; Chr.; Mar.; Died; Bur.; Parent Link Biological; Spouse

2. Sex M — Kenneth Ira Oakley
Born 18 Oct 1896 Place Butterfield,Missouri; Chr.; Mar.; Died; Bur.; Parent Link Biological; Spouse

3. Sex F — Gladys Lelia Oakley
Born 25 Jun 1899 Place Missouri; Chr.; Mar. Place; Died 4 Jun 1996 Place Centralia,Lewis,Washington,USA; Bur.; Parent Link Biological; Spouse Lee McEwen

4. Sex M — Oscar Oakley
Born abt 1905 Place Missouri; Chr.; Mar.; Died; Bur.; Parent Link Biological; Spouse

5. Sex — Name
Born; Chr.; Mar.; Died; Bur.; Spouse

Check here if other children are listed on additional pages.

Family Group Record   Francis Marion Oakley / Harriet Lovina Hazlett   6 Jan 2010   1 of 2
C:\My Documents\LEE & GLADYS MCEWEN.PAF

Husband's Name
Francis Marion Oakley

Born	11 Nov 1831	Place	Kentucky,USA
Chr.			
Mar.	9 Aug 1855	Place	Morgan County,Kentucky,USA
Died	8 May 1881	Place	Bond County,Illinois,USA
Bur.			

Father William Billy Oakley	Mother Martha S. Freeland	Parent Link Biological
Husband's other wives	Sidney Ellen Warner	

Wife's Name
Harriet Lovina Hazlett

Born	28 Oct 1833	Place	Indiana
Chr.			
Died	1 Oct 1875	Place	Toledo,Cumberland,Illinois,USA
Bur.			

Father	Mother	Parent Link
Wife's other husbands		

Children

1.Sex F	Name Martha Jane Oakley	
	Born 25 May 1858	Place
	Chr.	
	Mar.	
	Died 5 Jul 1936	Place
	Bur.	Parent Link Biological
	Spouse	

2.Sex M	Name William George Oscar Oakley	
	Born 23 Nov 1859	Place
	Chr.	
	Mar.	
	Died 29 Oct 1950	Place
	Bur.	Parent Link Biological
	Spouse	

3.Sex F	Name Laura Samantha Oakley	
	Born 10 Sep 1862	Place
	Chr.	
	Mar.	
	Died 24 Aug 1864	Place
	Bur.	Parent Link Biological
	Spouse	

4.Sex F	Name Lucinda Elzora Oakley	
	Born 22 Nov 1865	Place
	Chr.	
	Mar.	
	Died 30 Dec 1939	Place
	Bur.	Parent Link Biological
	Spouse	

5.Sex F	Name Flora Belle Oakley	
	Born 19 May 1867	Place
	Chr.	
	Mar.	
	Died 11 Mar 1901	Place
	Bur.	Parent Link Biological
	Spouse	

☒ Check here if other children are listed on additional pages.

Husband	Francis Marion Oakley	Yr. of Birth 1831
Wife	Harriet Lovina Hazlett	Yr. of Birth 1833

Children (continued)

6. Sex M — Melvin Edwin Oakley

Born	4 Oct 1869	Place Toledo, Cumberland, Illinois, USA
Chr.		
Mar.	25 Sep 1892	Place
Died	11 Jan 1951	Place Benkelman, Dundy, Nebraska, USA
Bur.		Parent Link Biological
Spouse	Lillis Maude Tibbetts	

7. Sex F — Harriet Lovina Oakley

Born	29 Jul 1872	Place
Chr.		
Mar.		
Died	19 Jul 1912	Place
Bur.		Parent Link Biological
Spouse		

(Children 8–12 blank)

Husband	Francis Marion Oakley

Other Marriages:
Sidney Ellen Warner   Place

Family Group Record

Husband's Name: Francis Marion Oakley

Born	11 Nov 1831	Place Kentucky, USA
Chr.		
Mar.		Place
Died	8 May 1881	Place Bond County, Illinois, USA
Bur.		
Father William Billy Oakley	Mother Martha S. Freeland	Parent Link Biological
Husband's other wives	Harriet Lovina Hazlett	

Wife's Name: Sidney Ellen Warner

Born	13 Jun 1833	Place
Chr.		
Died	28 Jun 1854	Place Waverly, Morgan, Indiana, USA
Bur.		
Father	Mother	Parent Link
Wife's other husbands		

Children

1. Sex M Name: James Pleasant Oakley

Born	14 Jun 1854	Place
Chr.		
Mar.		
Died	25 Dec 1930	Place
Bur.		Parent Link Biological
Spouse		

2. Sex Name:

Born	
Chr.	
Mar.	
Died	
Bur.	
Spouse	

3. Sex Name:

Born	
Chr.	
Mar.	
Died	
Bur.	
Spouse	

4. Sex Name:

Born	
Chr.	
Mar.	
Died	
Bur.	
Spouse	

5. Sex Name:

Born	
Chr.	
Mar.	
Died	
Bur.	
Spouse	

☐ Check here if other children are listed on additional pages.

Husband Francis Marion Oakley

Other Marriages:
Harriet Lovina Hazlett
9 Aug 1855 Place Morgan County, Kentucky, USA

Family Group Record

William Billy Oakley / Martha S. Freeland
C:\My Documents\LEE & GLADYS MCEWEN.PAF

6 Jan 2010   1 of 3

Husband's Name: William Billy Oakley

Born	1797	Place Bath County, Kentucky, USA
Chr.		
Mar.	8 Mar 1819	Place Fleming County, Kentucky, USA
Died	aft 1870	Place Illinois
Bur.		

Father Christopher Oakley   Mother Rachel White   Parent Link Biological

Husband's other wives

Wife's Name: Martha S. Freeland

Born	1800	Place North Carolina, USA
Chr.		
Died	aft 1860	Place Illinois
Bur.		

Father   Mother   Parent Link

Wife's other husbands

Children

1. Sex M — Madison Crittenden Oakley

Born	11 Apr 1820	Place Kentucky, USA
Chr.		
Mar.		
Died	aft 1850	Place Illinois
Bur.		Parent Link Biological

Spouse

2. Sex M — John Franklin Oakley

Born	24 Jul 1821	Place Kentucky, USA
Chr.		
Mar.		
Died	29 Apr 1894	Place
Bur.		Parent Link Biological

Spouse

3. Sex F — Nancy Oakley

Born	17 Oct 1823	Place Kentucky, USA
Chr.		
Mar.		
Died		
Bur.		Parent Link Biological

Spouse

4. Sex F — Priscilla Oakley

Born	7 Mar 1827	Place Kentucky, USA
Chr.		
Mar.		
Died		
Bur.		Parent Link Biological

Spouse

5. Sex M — Pleasant E. Oakley

Born	5 Apr 1828	Place Kentucky, USA
Chr.		
Mar.		
Died	15 Mar 1874	Place Toledo, Cumberland, Illinois, USA
Bur.		Parent Link Biological

Spouse

☒ Check here if other children are listed on additional pages.

Family Group Record

William Billy Oakley / Martha S. Freeland
C:\My Documents\LEE & GLADYS MCEWEN.PAF

6 Jan 2010

Husband	William Billy Oakley	Yr. of Birth 1797
Wife	Martha S. Freeland	Yr. of Birth 1800

Children (continued)

6. Sex	Name		
M	William A. Oakley		
	Born 31 Jan 1830	Place Kentucky,USA	
	Chr.		
	Mar.		
	Died		
	Bur.		Parent Link Biological
	Spouse		

7. Sex	Name		
M	Francis Marion Oakley		
	Born 11 Nov 1831	Place Kentucky,USA	
	Chr.		
	Mar.	Place	
	Died 8 May 1881	Place Bond County,Illinois,USA	
	Bur.		Parent Link Biological
	Spouse Sidney Ellen Warner	There are other marriage(s)	

8. Sex	Name		
F	Milly Ann Oakley		
	Born 2 Mar 1833	Place Bath County,Kentucky,USA	
	Chr.		
	Mar.		
	Died aft 1874	Place Illinois	
	Bur.		Parent Link Biological
	Spouse		

9. Sex	Name		
F	Emily M. Oakley		
	Born 1 Feb 1835	Place	
	Chr.		
	Mar.		
	Died		
	Bur.		Parent Link Biological
	Spouse		

10. Sex	Name		
	Born		
	Chr.		
	Mar.		
	Died		
	Bur.		
	Spouse		

11. Sex	Name		
	Born		
	Chr.		
	Mar.		
	Died		
	Bur.		
	Spouse		

12. Sex	Name		
	Born		
	Chr.		
	Mar.		
	Died		
	Bur.		
	Spouse		

Husband	William Billy Oakley

Notes for William Billy Oakley:

William and his wife Martha with their children went to Indiana about 1852, in 1863 they migrated to Illinois. It is said that William raised the 2 children that his sister Mary Polly had after she died.

Family Group Record

William Billy Oakley / Martha S. Freeland
C:\My Documents\LEE & GLADYS MCEWEN.PAF

6 Jan 2010

Child 7	Francis Marion Oakley

Other Marriages:

Harriet Lovina Hazlett
9 Aug 1855   Place Morgan County, Kentucky, USA

Family Group Record William S. Parkinson / Nancy C. Morris 6 Jan 2010
C:\My Documents\LEE & GLADYS MCEWEN.PAF

Husband's Name
William S. Parkinson

Born	21 Apr 1823	Place New York,USA	
Chr.			
Mar.	8 Jan 1845	Place Porter County, Indiana,USA	
Died	24 Feb 1870	Place Westville,La Porte,Indiana	
Bur.			
Father		Mother	Parent Link

Husband's other wives

Wife's Name
Nancy C. Morris

Born	abt 1856	Place Ohio,USA	
Chr.			
Died			
Bur.			
Father		Mother	Parent Link

Wife's other husbands

Children

1. Sex M — Name William H. Parkinson

Born	abt 1847	Place Illinois,USA	
Chr.			
Mar.			
Died			
Bur.			Parent Link Biological
Spouse			

2. Sex F — Name Mary Elizabeth Parkinson

Born	14 Aug 1851	Place Terre Haute, Vigo Co., In.	
Chr.			
Mar.	9 Mar 1869	Place Berrien Co., Mi.	
Died	20 Jul 1892	Place White Cloud, Doniphan Co., Ks.	
Bur.			Parent Link Biological
Spouse Horace Richard Titus			

3. Sex M — Name Geo G. Parkinson

Born	abt 1855	Place Illinois,USA	
Chr.			
Mar.			
Died			
Bur.			Parent Link Biological
Spouse			

4. Sex F — Name Charlena Parkinson

Born			
Chr.			
Mar.			
Died			
Bur.			Parent Link Biological
Spouse			

5. Sex — Name

Born			
Chr.			
Mar.			
Died			
Bur.			
Spouse			

☐ Check here if other children are listed on additional pages.

Husband   William S. Parkinson

Notes for William S. Parkinson:

William and Nancy Parkinson were on the 1860 New Durham, La Porte County, Michigan Federal Census, the Post Office was in Michigan City. William's occupation was a Stage Driver. His personal property was listed as $600.00. The census was taken on 3 July 1860, page number 138.

Stage Coach - Westville - Valparaiso

A tall man in a silk hat was the owner os a stage coach line between La Porte and Valparaiso. He was William S. Parkinson who lived at Westville and was born April 21, 1823 and died February 24, 1870. He was the father of Charlena Parkinson, who became the wife of E. E. Coddington - who was the father of Flossie M. Coddington.

La Porte Herald - August 20, 1915

The stage coach ended in the 1870's when Mr. Parkinson, who lived on Valparaiso Street in Westville, conducted the last stage route between Valparaiso and La Porte over the Jo;iet Road through Westville. He had the contract for carrying the mail and his low bid, combined with the falling off of passenger traffic due to the advent of buggies, put him out of business.

Burndea ~~Burnt by~~

The old MacEwen Castle was in Loch Fyne. The castle was ~~built by~~ the Campbell Clan. The Campbell clan massacred ~~the~~ MacDonald.

(MacEwen, MacLaghlans, MacNeills, and Campbells were all married to each other. Some McEwen married Campbell Ladies and McEwen Ladies married Campbell. One lives in Topeka, KS - McCune - Lady MaCampbell.

In 13th Century (Severa II, 1315- Gillespie V   they died four MacEwen sons Ewen VI, John VII, Walter VIII, Swene IX) last of the otter chiefs. There was a King Kenneth MacAlpin King in Dalriada 841 This clan came from Islay to Lock Fyne to Firth of Clyde - Ayr Culzean Castle - home of MacEwen. Some of the McDonald went to Lanark Canada 1823 and some Campbell and McEwen came to Canada. Some came to the U.S.A.

Lanark is a little town in Scotland around Glasgow, Helensburgh, Greenock, Pasley, Hamilton, Kilmarnock, Ayr Culzean Castle, down to DumFries and Galloway Atlantic Ocean - North Sea. A good book to read is the Scottish World.

Eoghain,na,h=Oitrich - MacEwen of Otter

(McCune) MacEwan, McEwan
(Shop name Comet 1812 had three horsepower engine, she covered 4 miles per hour, between Glasgow and Greenock. She was wrecked in 1820 off Craignish Pointin Argyllshire, (ship-Marjorie) 1823 (Shop Thermopy Iae 1868)
Robert Adam built the Culzean Castle in Alyrshire-MacEwen house.
East India Company (18th - 19th Centuries)
NorthWest Company 1783
Baptist Missionary Founded in England 1792

Book - IRELAND - A TERRIBLE BEAUTY - William Butler Yeats Easter 1916

Down through the centuries Dublin Castle held the administrative offices and served as residence for the Crown's highest representatives. The castle now functions as the state apartments of the Republic for ceremonial purposes, but odors of arrogance and duplicity linger on.

Bedford Tower above the former office of Heralds now house the Genealogical office. The Four courts
Thomas Cooley and James Gandon are credited with lion's share of the public buildings which sprouted up at the end of the 18th century. Begun by the former and completed by the latter. The Four Courts on Inns Quay stands stately on the banks of the river Liffey. When it was seized by Anti-Treaty forces in 1922 the interior was badly damaged. The restored building houses the barristers' law library and a number of registrior as well as the Supreme and High Courts, The original Four Courts Exchequer, King's Bench, Chancery, and Common Pleas - Fathered the British character of Irish law, which scarcely differs today.
Doubleday & Company, Inc. Garden City, NY

Dublin Castle was Burnded in a war - 1922

Send Back

Copy send Back

107

Eva Titus, Charley Clark
Little boy, Vernon (Wm) Richard b: Jan 31, 1903
Oldest sister Lillian (Veva) M. Clark b: Nov 6, 1897, Nemaha, NB d: Feb 27, 1974

Mary J. Venn, William Titus Family
Girl is Esther, White Cloud, KS

Are Great Grandfather Richard Titus

Aar Great, Great Grandparents Liredin, CO
Marie E DeClute, Horace W. Titus
Daughter Eliza Ann (Lida) Selba
Are Great Great Aunt Richard-sister

Evelyn Pearl McEwen
Age 18, Aug 1922

Handwritten McEwens Record

⊐

Handwritten record found at George McEwen residence

"George Rex McEwen was born in Glasgow, Scotland on June 2nd, 1823, Died May 10, 1910. First came to U.S.A. looking for a younger brother and stopped in Chicago *Andrew called Sandy* and Wisconsin, returning to Scotland for a few years. The second time came to Canada, settled at Carlton, Lenrick, Co., Ontario and married there to Sarah Elizabeth Brindel, (born in 1830?, in Dublin, Ireland, died Nov. 15, 1913) daughter of Lord John Brindel of the House of Parliament of Nana, Tipperary Co., Ireland, (Sarah is our great-grandmother. She ran away from her home in Ireland. She was a stowaway and all she had to eat were cookies during her trip to Ontario. She was 11 years old at the time.) His first marriage was to Miss McMahan, and after his first wife's death — he married again, but do not know here name. (Sarah was his third wife?)

George and Sarah
1. Isabella married 1) Ed Cronan, son Edwin
                     2) George Comer, daughter Ida, son George
                     3) Andrew Minard
2. Sarah Elizabeth married John Edward Parker, son John, Jr.
3. John born 12-18-1851 in Carleton, Ontario, Canada. Married Mary Etta Rowley.
   > Infant son died July 14, 1881 at birth
   > Lewis Elmer born March 7, 1883 - 4 miles east of Republic, KS. d. 1-8-1952. Married Ether Nina Harsh 10-5-1905, born 2-17-1885, d 4-22-1960.
   > Leonard Russell
   > Bertha May born March 2, 1887 - 2 miles east of Republic, KS Married Arthur Emmert.
   > Sylvia O'Resta born March 22, 1894 - 4 miles east of Republic, KS died December 9, 1894.
   > Lawrence LeRoy born May 3, 1896, died 5-23-1961, married Ethel Gertrude Mitchell.
4. Margaret married Jessie Beers, son Issac Beers
5. George, single, cigar maker
6. Agnes married Alexander Cole, daughter Udona married John McNitt. Later Agnes married Williams.
7. Tom, died Sept. 15, 1930, Wichita Falls, TX. Married Millie (Quick?) Matalock.
   > Delbert married Helen Seeley
   > Sylva
   > Jessie
   > Christina
   > Max

DEC. 3 1 1991

2

McEwen

1st Gen.	Lord and Lady Brindle of Ireland
2nd Gen.	Daughter Brindle M. McEwen
1st Gen.	on Sarah Brindle - Father Lord John and Lady McMahan
3rd Gen.	the sons of Brindle and McEwen - 8 children
3rd Gen.	is our Great Grandfather

George Rex McEwen m. (Sarah E. Brindle) *Ireland* *my grand father - Elzora J McEwen*
12 children - 4th Gen. William McEwen

4th Gen. Brother —James Ivan McEwen b. 6-22-1868 in Des Moines, IA d. 9-29-1949 Wray (Yoma). CO.
m. 1st wife Belle Bliss (dive) b. 1876, Washington, KS. died age 32 heart attack - her 2nd m. Hamer Catrell 3-12-02, Wabaunsee Co., KS - her father Thomas Hill - Mother Emma - 1 son -

5th Gen. Alva Merritt McEwen b. 4-1-1896 in Byron, NE. d. Burlingame, KS. 1st wife Marie Sheppard - 2nd wife Doris Wollever 5-5-32 Topeka, KS. b. 4-6-1808 d. 4-15-81. Alva died 12-16-59 Burlingame, KS - 1 daughter

6th Gen. Carol Lee McEwen b. 5-27-36 Topeka, KS. m. Dale Stout 5-23-54 Burlingame, KS 2 children - 7th Gen.

7th Gen. Teresa Lynne Stout b. 6-15-1955 m. Mitch Saunders 7-23-77 - 2 children - 8th Gen.
Kevin D. Stout b. 12-28-57 m. Sandra C. Lazzers 8-12-78 - 3 children - 8th Gen.

4th Gen. James Ivan McEwen 2nd wife Mary Ardella "Dello" Brittain. b. 4-30-1882 Alva, OK d. 10-27-69 in Wray CO - her father Orlando Brittain. Mother Jenetie Frost.

5th Gen. 12 children

5th Gen. 1st Son Clarence Ray McEwen b. 3-9-1901 m. Louise Berndt - children? 6th Gen.
2nd Son Leroy Ralph "Jack" McEwen b. 9-13-1904 still alive 1992 had a massive stroke.
1st wife Edna Cox 3-31-1936 - 6 children 6th gen.
2nd wife Marge Stinsen 3rd wife Hazel Sturdevant

6th Gen. 1. Mildred McEwen 2. Donna McEwen Karvia 3. Milford (Mel) McEwen 4. LeRoy (died) 5. Melvin McEwen 6. Dale McEwen
Donna McEwen m. John Karvia - 3 sons (7th gen.)
1. Patrick Karvia 2. Jack Karvia 3. Mike Karvia

5th Gen. Claude Orville McEwen b. 11-27-1908 d. ? m. 1. Ruby Coil —died in house fire. 2. Gladys 3. Louise Berndt McEwen (former wife of brother Clarence who left his family).

-1-

Ancestral File (TM) - ver 4.10   PEDIGREE CHART   08 SEP 1993   Chart 2

No. 1 on this chart is the same as no. 16 on chart no. 1

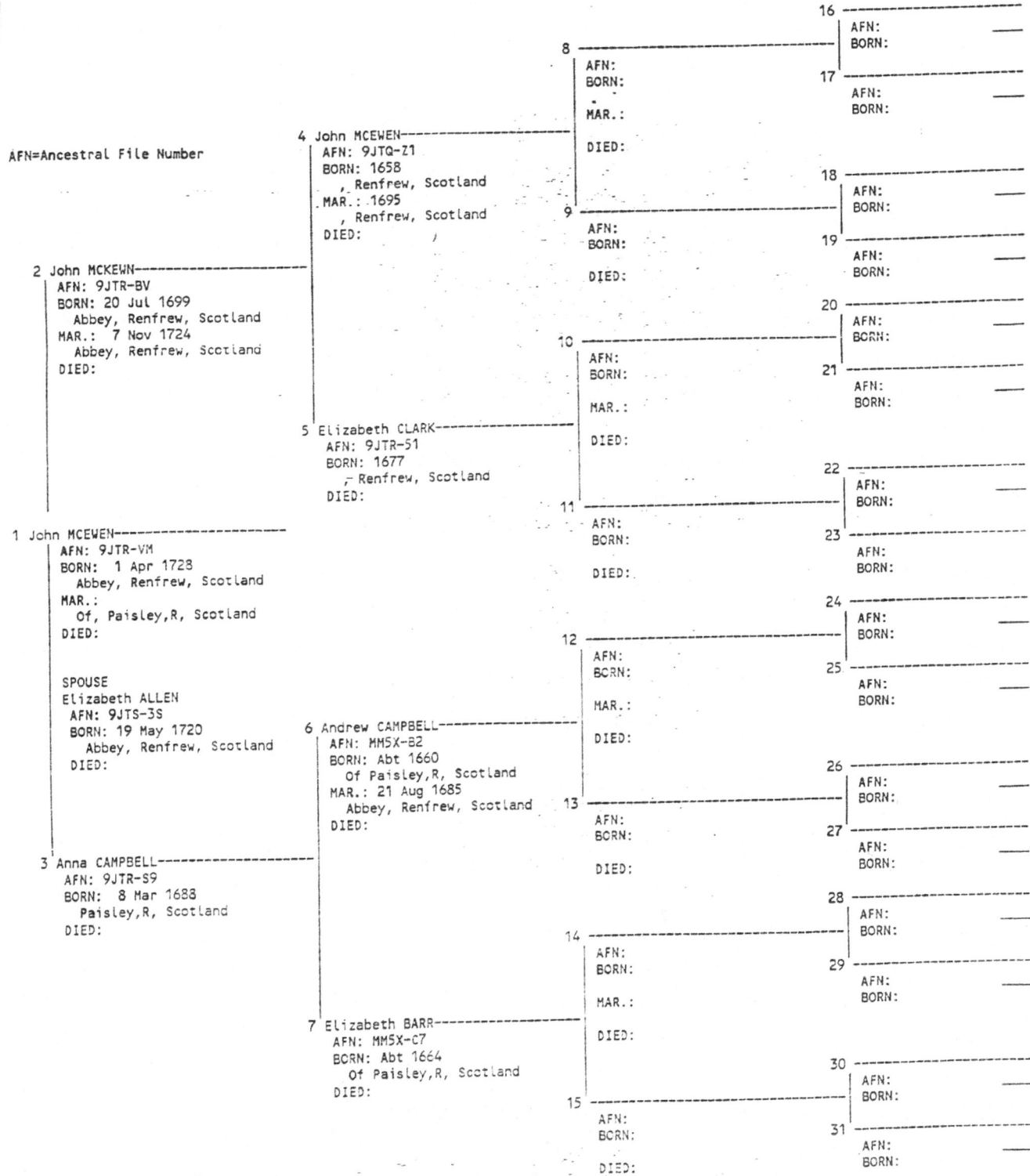

```
                                                                      16 --------------
                                                                        AFN:        ___
                                                     8 -------------     BORN:
                                                       AFN:              17 --------------
                                                       BORN:               AFN:       ___
                                                       MAR.:               BORN:
AFN=Ancestral File Number              4 John MCEWEN----   DIED:
                                         AFN: 9JTQ-Z1                     18 --------------
                                         BORN: 1658                        AFN:       ___
                                           , Renfrew, Scotland             BORN:
                                         MAR.: 1695
                                           , Renfrew, Scotland  9 --------------  19 --------------
                                         DIED:          /       AFN:               AFN:       ___
                                                               BORN:               BORN:
  2 John MCKEWN----------------------                DIED:
    AFN: 9JTR-BV                                                         20 --------------
    BORN: 20 Jul 1699                                                      AFN:       ___
      Abbey, Renfrew, Scotland           10 --------------                 BORN:
    MAR.: 7 Nov 1724                       AFN:                           21 --------------
      Abbey, Renfrew, Scotland            BORN:                            AFN:       ___
    DIED:                                  MAR.:                           BORN:
                                     5 Elizabeth CLARK----   DIED:
                                       AFN: 9JTR-51
                                       BORN: 1677                        22 --------------
                                         , Renfrew, Scotland               AFN:       ___
                                       DIED:          11 --------------    BORN:
                                                       AFN:              23 --------------
  1 John MCEWEN-----------------------                 BORN:              AFN:       ___
    AFN: 9JTR-VM                                       DIED:               BORN:
    BORN: 1 Apr 1728
      Abbey, Renfrew, Scotland                                          24 --------------
    MAR.:                                                                  AFN:       ___
      Of, Paisley,R, Scotland            12 --------------                 BORN:
    DIED:                                  AFN:                           25 --------------
                                          BORN:                            AFN:       ___
    SPOUSE                                 MAR.:                           BORN:
    Elizabeth ALLEN                   6 Andrew CAMPBELL----   DIED:
      AFN: 9JTS-3S                      AFN: MM5X-B2
      BORN: 19 May 1720                 BORN: Abt 1660                   26 --------------
        Abbey, Renfrew, Scotland          Of Paisley,R, Scotland          AFN:       ___
      DIED:                             MAR.: 21 Aug 1685                  BORN:
                                          Abbey, Renfrew, Scotland 13 --  27 --------------
                                        DIED:          AFN:               AFN:       ___
                                                      BORN:               BORN:
  3 Anna CAMPBELL---------------------                DIED:
    AFN: 9JTR-S9                                                        28 --------------
    BORN: 8 Mar 1688                                                      AFN:       ___
      Paisley,R, Scotland               14 --------------                 BORN:
    DIED:                                  AFN:                           29 --------------
                                          BORN:                            AFN:       ___
                                           MAR.:                           BORN:
                                     7 Elizabeth BARR------   DIED:
                                       AFN: MM5X-C7
                                       BORN: Abt 1664                    30 --------------
                                         Of Paisley,R, Scotland           AFN:       ___
                                       DIED:          15 --------------    BORN:
                                                       AFN:              31 --------------
                                                      BORN:               AFN:       ___
                                                      DIED:               BORN:
```

Copyright © 1987, July 1992 by The Church of Jesus Christ of Latter-day Saints. All rights reserved.

whatever, and particularly to _____

of whom he was heretofore a subject.

Sworn to and subscribed before me this ____ 7 ____ day of ____ October ____ 1872.

(SEAL OF COURT.) _____ _____ Clerk.

By _____ M. L. Reid _____, Deputy Clerk.

UNITED STATES OF AMERICA.

State of Kansas
Cloud County. ss.

Before the Clerk of the District Court of the Twelfth Judicial District of said State, personally appeared ____ George McCormick ____, a native of _____, aged about ____ 41 ____ years, who being duly sworn upon his oath declares that it is bona fide his intention to become a citizen of the United States of North America, and to renounce and abjure forever all allegiance and fidelity to every foreign power, prince, potentate, state and sovereignty, whatever, and particularly to _____ of whom he was heretofore a subject.

British Dominion

Sworn to and subscribed before me this ____ 14 ____ day of ____ October ____ 1872.

George McCormick

(SEAL OF COURT.) _____

By ____ Wm L Reid ____ Clerk.

M. L. Reid, Deputy Clerk.

cestral File (TM) - ver 4.10

N.A. are Slides

PEDIGREE CHART

08 SEP 1993   Chart _1_

. 1 on this chart is the same as no. _____ on chart no. _____

N=Ancestral File Number

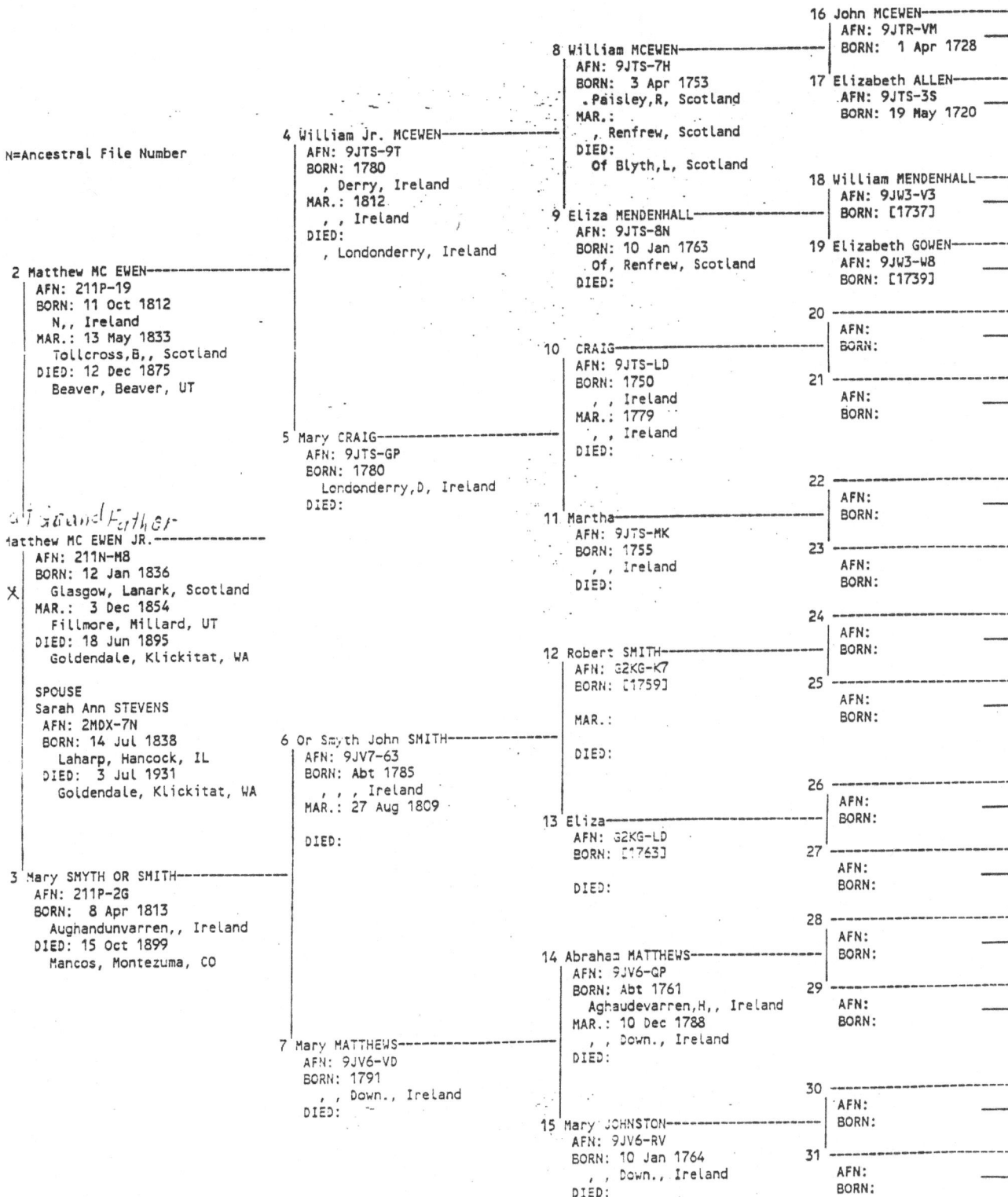

2 Matthew MC EWEN
AFN: 211P-19
BORN: 11 Oct 1812
N,, Ireland
MAR.: 13 May 1833
Tollcross,B,, Scotland
DIED: 12 Dec 1875
Beaver, Beaver, UT

at Grand Father

Matthew MC EWEN JR.
AFN: 211N-M8
BORN: 12 Jan 1836
X Glasgow, Lanark, Scotland
MAR.: 3 Dec 1854
Fillmore, Millard, UT
DIED: 18 Jun 1895
Goldendale, Klickitat, WA

SPOUSE
Sarah Ann STEVENS
AFN: 2MDX-7N
BORN: 14 Jul 1838
Laharp, Hancock, IL
DIED: 3 Jul 1931
Goldendale, Klickitat, WA

3 Mary SMYTH OR SMITH
AFN: 211P-2G
BORN: 8 Apr 1813
Aughandunvarren,, Ireland
DIED: 15 Oct 1899
Mancos, Montezuma, CO

4 William Jr. MCEWEN
AFN: 9JTS-9T
BORN: 1780
, Derry, Ireland
MAR.: 1812
, , Ireland
DIED:
, Londonderry, Ireland

5 Mary CRAIG
AFN: 9JTS-GP
BORN: 1780
Londonderry,D, Ireland
DIED:

6 Or Smyth John SMITH
AFN: 9JV7-63
BORN: Abt 1785
, , , Ireland
MAR.: 27 Aug 1809
DIED:

7 Mary MATTHEWS
AFN: 9JV6-VD
BORN: 1791
, , Down., Ireland
DIED:

8 William MCEWEN
AFN: 9JTS-7H
BORN: 3 Apr 1753
.Paisley,R, Scotland
MAR.:
, Renfrew, Scotland
DIED:
Of Blyth,L, Scotland

9 Eliza MENDENHALL
AFN: 9JTS-8N
BORN: 10 Jan 1763
.Of, Renfrew, Scotland
DIED:

10 CRAIG
AFN: 9JTS-LD
BORN: 1750
, , Ireland
MAR.: 1779
, , Ireland
DIED:

11 Martha
AFN: 9JTS-MK
BORN: 1755
, , Ireland
DIED:

12 Robert SMITH
AFN: G2KG-K7
BORN: [1759]
MAR.:
DIED:

13 Eliza
AFN: G2KG-LD
BORN: [1763]
DIED:

14 Abraham MATTHEWS
AFN: 9JV6-QP
BORN: Abt 1761
Aghaudevarren,H,, Ireland
MAR.: 10 Dec 1788
, , Down., Ireland
DIED:

15 Mary JOHNSTON
AFN: 9JV6-RV
BORN: 10 Jan 1764
, , Down., Ireland
DIED:

16 John MCEWEN
AFN: 9JTR-VM
BORN: 1 Apr 1728

17 Elizabeth ALLEN
AFN: 9JTS-3S
BORN: 19 May 1720

18 William MENDENHALL
AFN: 9JW3-V3
BORN: [1737]

19 Elizabeth GOWEN
AFN: 9JW3-W8
BORN: [1739]

20
AFN:
BORN:

21
AFN:
BORN:

22
AFN:
BORN:

23
AFN:
BORN:

24
AFN:
BORN:

25
AFN:
BORN:

26
AFN:
BORN:

27
AFN:
BORN:

28
AFN:
BORN:

29
AFN:
BORN:

30
AFN:
BORN:

31
AFN:
BORN:

.right © 1987, July 1992 by The Church of Jesus Christ of Latter-day Saints. All rights reserved.

Earl McEwen H.3621, Old Hwy B. Morgan UT 84050 Tel 1-801-8

7

                        James McEwen & Belle Bliss
                            (4th Generation)

James McEwen   b. 6-22-1868 Des Moines, Iowa
                    d. 9-29-1949 Wray, CO
                    m. Belle Bliss   b. 1876 in Washington, KS
                                      d. age 32- heart attack-bur. Harveyville, KS
                          father - Thomas Bliss
                          mother - Emma Hill Bliss
                        children:
                        Alva Merritt McEwen   b. 4-1-1897 Nebraska

James & Belle were divorced before Alva was 2 years old.
        Belle married Homer Cantrell on 3-12-02. They lived in Wabaunsee Co., KS
        Belle is buried at the cemetery in Harveyville, KS

Alva first married to Marie Sheppard Lloyd.
married Doris E. Welliever on 5-5-35 at Topeka, KS. Doris died 4-15-81 in
Burlingame, KS.
Alva & Doris had one daughter
        Carol Lee McEwen   b. 5-27-36 in Topeka, KS
                            d.
                            m. Dale H. Stout 5-23-54 at Burlingame, KS
            children: Teresa Lynne Stout   b. 6-15-55
                                               d.
                                               m. Mitch Saunders 7-23-1977
                            children: Nicholas Ryan Saunders b. 9-25-80
                                       Brock Alan Saunders   b. 11-23-1982
                                       They live in Topeka, KS
                       Kevin Douglas Stout   b. 12-28-1957
                                               d.
                                               m. Sandra C. Lazzers 8-12-1978
                            children: Brett Steven Stout   b. 9-29-1980
                                       Kyle Douglas Stout   b. 2-14-1984
                                       Lauren Denae Stout   b. 10-31-1987
                                       They live in Topeka, KS

James McEwen m. Mary Ardella "Della" Brittain
                    b. 4-30-1882, Alva, OK
                    d. 10-27-1969 Wray (Yuma) Col.
                        buried 10-29-1969 Grandview Cemetery
                        father Orlando Brittain
                        mother Jenetke Frost
                        11 children
                    children:
        X Clarence Ray   b. 3-9-1901   d.
                                     m. Louise Berndt
          LeRoy Ralph "Jack"   b. 9-13-1904   d.
                                     m. 1. Edna Cox 3-31-1936
                                        2. Marge Stinsen
                                        3. Hazel Sturdevant
          Floyd Harold "Bud"   b. 11-13-1905 Indianola, NE
                                     d. 7-9-1984 (ashes over Cascade
                                        Mountains)
                                     m. Florina Kistler 10-29-1929
                                     m. Lorraine 5-27-1957
          Clifford Arnold   b. 5-1-1906   d. bur. Wray, CO
                                     m. Edna Castle
          Claude Orville   b. 11-27-1908
                                     m. 1. Ruby Coil d. house fire 2. Gladys
                                        3. Louise Berndt McEwen bur-Portland -Or
          Alta Irene "Billie"   b. 12-11-1910 Indianola, NE
                                     m. Albert Zick 1939 (Div.)

T-1-S - THayer Co NEB - WASHINGTON R-4-W
Hi 25 - Hubbell - Reynolds - Fairbury

Land
James William ↤
And Agnes McEwen ↓

HARBINE   willis   R.Walter   Junior Hoops   John Young Jr

Vernon Grauerholz Har. 1 6	W-W H 5 Albert KiKager Byr 1	LaVer Car Mohrman Bohling Byr 4	Heitmann 3	2 1
7	Calvin seybold 8	Gene Fischer 9		
18	17	Ernest Kroeger 16	Harold Mitchell 15 22	14 Ralph L Morehead 23 13 24
19	20	21 Rahe - Rahe Frye	Brown	
30	29	Margaret Brown 28	27	26 George McEwen 25
			5½ SW 4	
Richard Barrett Rep. 1 31	Fred Hoops Rep.1 Dean Hobelmann 32	D.F Van Nortwick 33 Dana johnson	34	Donald McEwen Byr N½ 1 NW 35

BIG BEND TWP

LIBERTY of MY

Union

Land
George McEwen Section 26 and 35

Republic Ks 1981

7

James McEwen & Belle Bliss
(4th Generation)

James McEwen   b. 6-22-1868 Des Moines, Iowa
                       d. 9-29-1949 Wray, CO
                       m. Belle Bliss   b. 1876 in Washington, KS
                                         d. age 32- heart attack-bur. Harveyville, KS
                           father - Thomas Bliss
                           mother - Emma Hill Bliss
                     children:
                     Alva Merritt McEwen   b. 4-1-1897 Nebraska

James & Belle were divorced before Alva was 2 years old.
         Belle married Homer Cantrell on 3-12-02. They lived in Wabaunsee Co., KS
         Belle is burried at the cemetery in Harveyville, KS

Alva first married to Marie Sheppard Lloyd.
married Doris E. Welliever on 5-5-35 at Topeka, KS. Doris died 4-15-81 in Burlingame, KS.
Alva & Doris had one daughter
         Carol Lee McEwen   b. 5-27-36 in Topeka, KS
                                  d.
                                  m. Dale H. Stout 5-23-54 at Burlingame, KS
                children: **Teresa Lynne Stout**   b. 6-15-55
                                             d.
                                             m. Mitch Saunders 7-23-1977
                         children: Nicholas Ryan Saunders   b. 9-25-80
                                         Brock Alan Saunders   b. 11-23-1982
                                         They live in Topeka, KS
                         Kevin Douglas Stout   b. 12-28-1957
                                             d.
                                             m. Sandra C. Lazzers 8-12-1978
                         children: Brett Steven Stout   b. 9-29-1980
                                         Kyle Douglas Stout   b. 2-14-1984
                                         Lauren Denae Stout   b. 10-31-1987
                                         They live in Topeka, KS

James McEwen m. Mary Ardella "Della" Brittain
                     b. 4-30-1882, Alva, OK
                     d. 10-27-1969 Wray (Yuma) Col.
                         buried 10-29-1969 Grandview Cemetery
                         father Orlando Brittain
                         mother Jenetke Frost
                         11 children
                     children:
                     Clarence Ray   b. 3-9-1901   d.
                                         m. Louise Berndt
                     LeRoy Ralph "Jack"   b. 9-13-1904   d.
                                         m. 1. Edna Cox 3-31-1936
                                                2. Marge Stinsen
                                                3. Hazel Sturdevant
                     Floyd Harold "Bud"   b. 11-13-1905 Indianola, NE
                                         d. 7-9-1984 (ashes over Cascade
                                                Mountains)
                                         m. Florina Kistler 10-29-1929
                                         m. Lorraine 5-27-1957
                     Clifford Arnold   b. 5-1-1906   d. bur. Wray, CO
                                         m. Edna Castle
                     Claude Orville   b. 11-27-1908
                                         m. 1. Ruby Coil d. house fire 2. Gladys
                                                3. Louise Berndt McEwen
                     Alta Irene "Billie"   b. 12-11-1910 Indianola, NE
                                         m. Albert Zick 1939 (Div.)

Earl & Elsie had 8 children:
    Floyd
    Martha (deceased)
    Vera Liberty
    Ida Smith
    Elsie
    Georgia Hayes
    Gladys Gall
    Barbara _____ (Texas)

Ivan's first wife was Ruth Randall - they had 3 children:
    Ruth Elaine Hurley - Denver, CO
    William F. Titus - Falls City, NE
    Patricia D. Medeiros - Fresno, CA

Ivan married M. Marie Foster Ivey 9-26-40
  moved from Nebraska to Denver one week after marriage.

    Marie had one daughter:
    Rose Marie Ivey Governale
    Ivan & Marie have two children:

    Ivan Douglas Titus b. 4-25-1942, Pomona, CA
      married: Gail Rae Thomas 11-25-1961
      children: Ivan David Titus b. 1962
             Paul Douglas Titus b. 1975
             Gaylea Rose Titus Albrecht b. 1964
             Heather Dawn Titus Fant b. 1968
             Gennifer Hollie Titus Hoffman b. 1971

    Karen Myrtle Titus James b 6-21.1946
      married: Floyd E. James 12-5-1964, Amity, OR
      children: Shawn Eugene James
             Shannon Collen James Fisher

Between **Ivan** and **Marie** they have 17 grandchildren, 20 some great-grandchildren and great-great-grandchildren.

3

6th Gen.	Reta McEwen (dive)- George Emmett 2nd daughter Chartier McEwen m. Russ Clark -died, Chartier was a twin of Rex McEwen - died. 3rd daughter Evelyn McEwen Pilkington, 4th daughter Ruth Ann McEwen was in the house fire too, she is a paraplegic, 5th brother Claude McEwen, Jr. called Gunion, lives in Portland, Oregon. Reta, Chartier, Evelyn live in Ft. Collins, CO. Ruth A. McEwen lives at 1910 Broadway St., N. E., Salem, OR 97303 telephone 503-378-0895
5th Gen.	Alta Irene "Billie" McEwen b. 12-11-1910 Indianola, NE m. Albert Zick (div.) 1939. Billie was hospitalized with breathing difficulty. Stella Marie b. 10-2-1912 McCook, NE was 80 years old Oct. 2, 1992. m. Eldon Theadore Bahler on Easter Sunday, April 5, 1931 in Greeley, CO.
6th Gen.	Jimmie Lee Bahler b. 8-6-1937 d. 9-13-1939 Ray Eldon Bahler b. 9-25-1941 Holyoke, CO m. Betty Lou Fisbeck 1-12-1962 Holyoke, CO. 3 children 7th Gen.
7th Gen.	Michael Ray Bahler b. 8-14-1962 Holyoke, CO m. Beth Schneider 3-15-1980 (div.)
8th Gen.	Corey Ray Bahler b. 10-8-1980 Jeremy Wayne Bahler b. 10-18-1981
7th Gen.	Michael R. Bahler 2nd wife Barbara Ann Elder. Mike is a Nuclear Submarine Naval Officer living in Kittery, Maine
8th Gen.	Matthew Chase b.
7th Gen.	Launa Lynn Bahler b. 7-18-1963 Holyoke, CO m. Christopher Connon - live in Arvada, CO (Denver suburb)
8th Gen.	Brady Eldon Connon b. 3-25-1988 Danielle Kristine Connon b. 5-1991
7th Gen.	Wayne Allen Bahler b. 2-22-1970 - single - Working for a farmer at Gothenburg, NE
8th Gen.	Matthew Chase Bahler
6th Gen.	Richard Glen Bahler b. 12-26-1942 - Sterling, CO m. Ronnie Grace Watkins 3-16-1968 in Warrensburg, MO - 4 children -7th Gen.
7th Gen.	1. Roxanne Gail Bahler b. 7-11-1970 Holyoke, CO, 2. Rachel Gaylynn Bahler b. 6-29-1972 Calif. 3. Renee Ginny Bahler b. 5-14-1975 Holyoke, CO, 4. Rhonda Ginger Bahler b. 5-24-1976 Holyoke, CO 2 oldest girls are in college. 2 younger are in high school.
6th Gen.	Linda Lou Bahler b. 11-19-1947 Holyoke, CO. m. Ralph Edward Statz 6-5-1965 Chase Co. Lamar, NE 3 children-7th Gen.
7th Gen.	1. "Chip" Ralph Edward Statz, Jr. b. 3-8-1966 Imperial, NE 2. Robyn Elaine Statz b. 6-15-1968 Tucson, AZ m. Robert H. Wilson 6-18-1988 (Bob's 3 children live with their mother in AK) 3. Ralyn Eileen Statz b. 6-3-1971 Holyoke, CO
5th Gen.	Maxine Lorene McEwen's husband Harold Brenner is dying of lung/liver cancer. All still alive in 1992. *Harold -d- Nov -1993- Cancer*

-3-

Nora McEwen Hankey

Father - **William McEwen** b 3-25-1864 Darlington, Wisconsin

d 4-14-1954, Cherokee, OK

Married **Lana Titus** June 28, 1886

b 5-30-1872 - Odell, IL

d 7-08-1961 - Cherokee, OK

Children

Boy and Girl died

Perry   b 10-10-1890, White Cloud, KS

d 01-02-1982

Married Mable A. Curly November, 1911

Married Ethel Tousley (sp.?)

Nora   b 04-04-1892, White Cloud, KS

d 07-09-1989, Topeka, KS (Mount Hope Cemetery

Married Clyde Walton Hankey November 21, 1916, Cherokee, OK

b 01-30-1897, Haven, KS

d 12-07-1971, Topeka, KS (Mount Hope Cemetery)

Nora McEwen met Clyde Hankey during the fair 9-16-1916 at Amarita, OK. Were engaged during the meeting at the Church of Christ 10-24-1916, Tuesday evening.

Lee   b 12-04-1894, Butler, MO

d 10-11-1968 - Grand Junction, CO

Married Gladys Oakley

Stella   b 11-21-1896, Heath Po, KS

d 4-23-1982 Grand Junction CO, Orchard Mesa Cemt.

Married Ira Seeley December 27, 1918

Elsie   b 07-15-1898, Nebraska

d 12-19-1970 St. Joseph, MO

Married Ed Madearis April 23, 1920

Ted   b 11-14-1902, Driftwood, OK

d 02-12-1966 CedarVale, KS

Married Nellie Swingle December 27, 1919

Pearl   b 12-11-1903, Driftwood, OK

d 07-16-1989, Chicago, IL

Married Bill Jacobsen

Willie   b 06-02-1906, Driftwood, OK

d 3-27-1981, Oklahoma City, OK

Married Dorothy January 4, 1941

Lana   b 12-15-1908, Cherokee, OK

d

Married Clifford Brown July 2, 1929

-3-

Nora McEwen Hankey

Father - **William McEwen** b 3-25-1864 Drlington, Wisconsin

d 4-14-1954, Cherokee, OK

Married **Lana Titus** June 28, 1886 Mankato-ks

b 5-30-1872 - Odell, IL

d 7-08-1961 - Cherokee, OK

Children

Boy and Girl died

Perry   b 10-10-1890, White Cloud, KS

d 01-02-1982

Married Mable A. Corly November, 1911

Nora   b 04-04-1892, White Cloud, KS

d 07-09-1989, Topeka, KS (Mount Hope Cemetery)

Married Clyde Walton Hankey November 21, 1916, Cherokee, OK

b 01-30-1897, Haven, KS

d 12-07-1971, Topeka, KS (Mount Hope Cemetery)

Nora McEwen met Clyde Hankey during the fair 9-16-1916 at Amarita, OK. Were engaged during the meeting at the Church of Christ 10-24-1916, Tuesday evening.

Lee   b 12-04-1894, Hume, MO

d

Married Gladys Oakley

Stella   b 11-21-1896, Heath Po, KS

d

Married Ira Seeley December 27, 1918

Elsie   b 07-15-1898, Nebraska

d 12-19-1970

Married El Medearis April 23, 1920

Ted   b 11-14-1901, Driftwood, OK

d 02-12-1966

Married Nellie Swingle December 27, 1919

Pearl   b 12-11-1903, Driftwood, OK

d 07-16-1989, Chicago, IL

Married Bill Jacobsen

Willie   b 06-02-1906, Driftwood, OK

d

Married Dorothy   January 4, 1941

Lana   b 12-15-1908, Cherokee, OK

d

Married Clifford Brown July 2, 1929

1

[illegible] ary McEwen papers

Larry McEwen
603 East 5th Street
Hastings, NE 68901
October 7, 1993
1-402-463-2267

Mrs. Mary Hanky Orson
317 N.E. Grattan
Topeka KS 66616   Telephone: (913) 232-9505

Dear Mary,

I have not been feeling too good since we took our long-planned grand vacation this summer. We were gone 26 days and visited Colorado, Wyoming, Montana, Alberta Canada, British Columbia Canada, the Queen Charlotte Islands (110 miles by ferry into the Pacific Ocean--we could see Alaska from where we stayed two days there), Vancouver Island (about 480 miles south by ferry from the Queen Charlotte Islands), Washington State USA, Oregon, Idaho, Wyoming, and finally, back to Nebraska. I was sick about 2/3 of the time but with my wife, Charlotte's, help, we managed to have a wonderful time. It was the most beautiful trip I could have imagined. We were so far north on the Queen Charlotte Islands that one evening we were sitting on the balcony outside our room and watching the sun near the horizon at midnight. We saw many kinds of deer, two kinds of mountain goats, big-horn sheep, elk, bison, antelope, marmots, short-tailed weasels (which are nearly extinct), bald eagles, golden eagles, owls, porpoises, seals, sea-lions, and I am sure many other species of wild life which I can't recall right now. We saw them fishing for the "running salmon" and ate fresh seafood of many kinds--salmon, halibut, tuna, trout, dungeness crab, mussels, clams, and other kinds that I cannot recall right now. I gained too much weight and still haven't lost it even though I have been sick so much this summer.

I have found some more information about the McEwen line. First, the information about Carleton Place in Ontario, Canada is wrong as far as the county goes. It is not "Lenrick" County. It is "Lanark" county which is named after "Lanark" county in Scotland. I have written to a Genealogical Society to see what can be found about George Rex McEwen and/or Elizabeth Brindel (or Brindle) McEwen. Maybe I will hear from someone.

I need to give you some information about me so you will know something of my life. I gave you such sketchy information before. I, Larry Burdette McEwen, was born at 9:15 a.m. in Clay Center, Nebraska, on August 4, 1934. I married JoAnne L. Carlson on ~~October~~ 3, 1956 and to this union was born Diana Jo McEwen in Moline, Illinois, on November 28, 1957, and Sheila Jo McEwen in Geneseo, Illinois, on May 6, 1967. JoAnne and I divorced in May, 1975, and I married Charlotte Alloway McEwen, on February 14, 1978. I noticed that there were some mistakes about marriage dates and/or birth dates.

Before going on there is also an error about my sister, Geraldine Marie McEwen who was born in Springfield, Missouri on May 10, 1936. She married Bill Bottolfson in March, 1956 (not 1955 as shown on some of your records). I think the birthdates of her children are correct.

Lanark County in Scotland now in the region of ~~Strathclyde~~ Strathclyde
[illegible] Lanarkshire (shir") (Lan'ark) Strathclyde SW Scotland on the Firth
[illegible] including the former counties of Ayr, Lanark, Renfrew and

White Cloud, KS
Methodist Church 6/25/92

White Cloud, KS 6/25/92

Highland, KS Methodist Church
6/25/92

White Cloud, KS /
Loise Rodecap Store
Esther Rodecap daughter.
Elrod Cemetery

John and Mary McEwen's son

Lawrence LeRoy McEwen
b: 3/3/1896, d: 5/23/1961
Washington Ccr
Republic, KS 1877

Perry McEwen M Mable Cerly, Nov 14, 1911, Oldest Child
Perry was a Penticostal Grace Preacher all over the country.

1st son Walter and June McEwen at Jackes house 1977

Feb 25-18-26   Esther A. Titus

George Rodecap – bur-here
and baby bur here   6-25-92

Esther Titus Rodecap

In Cemt
White Cloud KS
6-25-92
Lana and William – Fest – Children
Buried here – Roy, Maudie McEwen

Eva Titus Clark, Edward Titus, William Titus, Lana Ann Titus McEwen

Mary E. Parkinson, Richard-Toot Lowhon, Richard Titus
Baby is buried with her.

Nora McEwen -Hankey
Grand Father

Grand Mother
Sarah #E. Brindel-McEwen
Daughter of Lord John Brindel
Lady McMahan-Brindel of Ireland

George Rex McEwen
b. June 2, 1823
Glasgow, Scotland in the Places
7 Brothers
d. May 10, 1910,
Buried in Washington Cemt. KS
86 years old

Sarah Elizabeth Brindel
b. 1830 – Dublin, Ireland
Come to Ontario Canada at the age of
11 years old as a stowaway. 1841
d. November 15, 1913- 83 years old
Buried in Washington Cemt. KS

George Rex McEwen m. Sarah E. Brindel
In Carleton, Henrick Co. Ontario, Canada
Two daughters and a son born here
George & Sarah McEwen come to USA – 8 children born here.
Homestead: May 20, 1862. Republic, KS
The 8th child – William McEwen and Lana Ann Titus married, June 28, 1846, KS
11 children born.

Lana Titus McEwen & William McEwen
Grandmother and Grandfather of Zoula McEwen Wasik

Died 1910, 87 years old | Died Nov 15, 1913 83 years old

Family History

Family History

<u>Mom's Side Of Family:</u> English, Irish, Scottish, French, Italian, Swedish, Norwegian, Jewish, German, Netherlands

<u>Dad's Side Of Family:</u> English, Irish, Spanish, Italian, German, French, Jewish, Netherlands, Swedish

Last Names For The Golden Family

1.	Bond -	English
2.	Ayers -	English
3.	Temple -	English, French
4.	Friddle -	Netherlands, German, Jewish, Swedish
5.	Dibert -	German
6.	Fickes -	German
7.	Garver -	German
8.	Elting -	German
9.	Eckert -	German
10.	Ploeg -	Netherlands, Belgium
11.	Presselaar -	Netherlands, German, Jewish
12.	Sherwood -	English, possibly Jewish
13.	Freer -	English, French, German
14.	Rouw -	Netherlands, Belgium, English
15.	Ickes -	English, German
16.	LeRoy -	French
17.	Habig -	German
18.	Lambertse -	Netherlands possibly
19.	Click -	English
20.	Neely -	Irish
21.	Schafer -	German
22.	Peter -	English, German, Scottish, Nether., possibly Jewish
23.	Low -	English, Scottish
24.	Brink -	Netherlands, German, Danish, Swedish
25.	Catharina -	Netherlands
26.	Egbertz -	English
27.	DuBois -	French, English
28.	Golden -	English, Irish
29.	Stimers -	German-Jewish
30.	Wygant -	German, English possibly
31.	Blanshan -	French
32.	DeBart	Italian

Mystery Last Names????

1. Nei
2. Ickesh
3. Gerritson

Last Names For Mom's Family

1. Brindle - — English
2. Brush - — English
3. Carter - — English, French
4. Conklin – — Irish or Netherlands
5. DeClute - — possibly French or English
6. Dow - — English, Irish, Scottish
7. Freeland - — English
8. Gilson - — English
9. Hazlett - *Delated to HAZ* — English
10. Huntley - *cherry in Kent* — English
11. Lisaught - *WA.* — Irish
12. Mc Ewen - — Scottish
13. Oakley - — English
14. Parkinson - — English
15. Powers - — French, English
16. Robbins - — English, maybe Scottish
17. Scudder - — English, French, Netherlands
18. Smith - — English
19. Tibbets - — French, German, English
20. Titus - — Italian
21. Warner - — German, English
22. Young - — English, Irish, Scottish
23. White - — English, Irish
24. De Wolfe — German
25. Curle - — English
26. Mc Brune — ?????

Long Distance Family History For The Golden Family

1. Africa
2. Saudi Arabia (by the Red Sea)
3. Iraq
4. Iran
5. ~~Pakistan~~ or India
6. Kazakhstan
7. Papua New Guinea
8. Philippines (possibly Bohol Island)
9. Xinjiang, China (Taklimakan Desert Area)
10. Kazakhstan or Russia
11. Russia
12. England
13. Spain
14. Italy
15. France (showed no arrow, but showed a marker)
16. Germany (showed no arrow, but showed a marker)

Notes: They showed no arrow for Netherlands, but they are doing research on one or more of the markers. One of the markers is the M-222 which is the last marker. There are last names for Netherlands on the names list and one had a first name that also looked like it was Netherlands.

Mom's Long Distant Family History

1. Africa
2. Saudi Arabia (by the upper part of the Red Sea)
3. Yemen (by the lower part of the Red Sea)
4. Turkey
5. Russia
6. Iran
7. Saudi Arabia by Riyadh
8. India
9. Kazakhstan
10. Ukraine or Russia
11. Russia
12. Norway or Sweden
13. Poland
14. Russia
15. Russia
16. Sweden
17. Italy
18. France
19. England
20. Russia

fishing
6 Sarah
3 Dine Jessica & Hay
3 Clove
7 Cheryl
2 Bob Vici
2 Donna
23
about 40 at Lake
Diane's

Introduction

TITUS FAMILY

GENEALOGY

HOME ARTICLES INDEX CENSUS OBITS VITAL STATS TRAVEL

BRICK WALLS DNA NEWS CONTACT FEEDBACK

Are-Grart Grart, Graet-Garnd Frathr

Nominal Index to the U.S. Titus Genealogy

Generation Number	Name	Database Reference	Relationship
8	Titus, Horace W.	473	h/o Mary A. Swett 2nd ?
8	Titus, Horace W.	473	h/o Maria DeClute 3nd

1st

Introduction

ALVIN PEARL TITUS

My motivation for research into the Titus family stemmed initially from the fact that my mother, Vera (nee Titus), was part of the lineage. However, once I became more involved in the research, and the various historical, political and social elements began to unfold over the 350-plus years of living history covered in my search, I became more and more fascinated, more and more involved with the numerous and varied cast of characters.

These people, particularly the descendants of Robert Titus, are my relatives and my ancestors. They are, and were, simple, hard-working and God-fearing folk. They are mainly farmers and labourers, with a sprinkling of shopkeepers, school teachers and clergymen. They have remained in that humble social status for much of the 350 years that they have contributed to and woven the fabric of North America. Only in the past 70 or 80 years do we find significant representation in the sciences, the arts or the senior ranks of the military. In religion, they are mostly Protestants, with the Baptist, Quaker and Methodist Churches being their preferred houses of worship.

Titn — Titus

Send Back Cope

http://www.titusfamily.ca/index.php?option=com_content&view=article&id=1:introduction&catid=1:home 4/24/2

THE McEWEN FAMILY

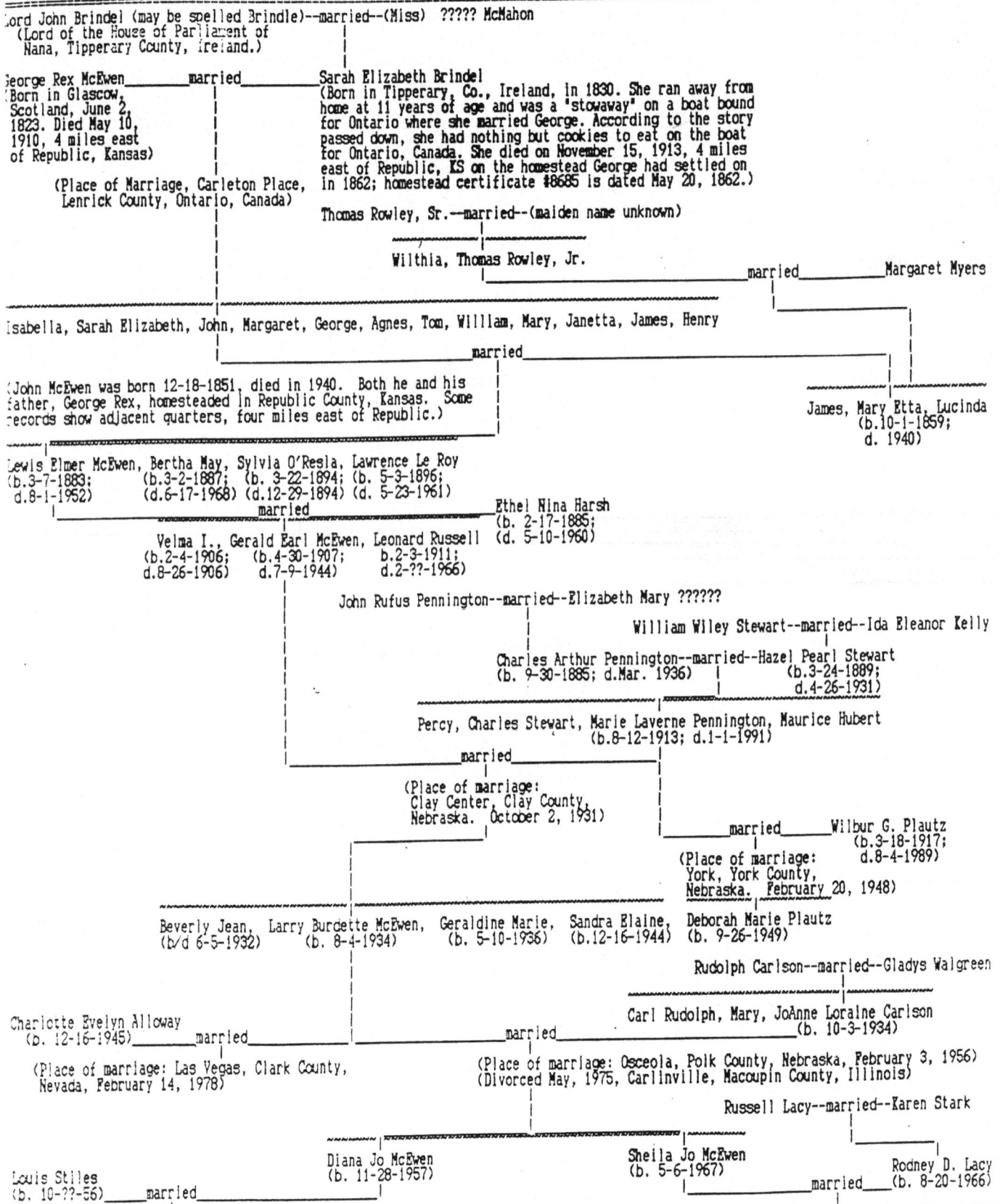

Lord John Brindel (may be spelled Brindle)--married--(Miss) ????? McMahon
(Lord of the House of Parliament of
Nana, Tipperary County, Ireland.)

George Rex McEwen_____married_____ Sarah Elizabeth Brindel
(Born in Glascow,   (Born in Tipperary, Co., Ireland, in 1830. She ran away from
Scotland, June 2,   home at 11 years of age and was a "stowaway" on a boat bound
1823. Died May 10,   for Ontario where she married George. According to the story
1910, 4 miles east   passed down, she had nothing but cookies to eat on the boat
of Republic, Kansas)   for Ontario, Canada. She died on November 15, 1913, 4 miles
                                                 east of Republic, KS on the homestead George had settled on
        (Place of Marriage, Carleton Place,   in 1862; homestead certificate #8685 is dated May 20, 1862.)
        Lenrick County, Ontario, Canada)
                                                 Thomas Rowley, Sr.--married--(maiden name unknown)

                                                        Wilthia, Thomas Rowley, Jr.
                                                                                                    married_____ Margaret Myers

Isabella, Sarah Elizabeth, John, Margaret, George, Agnes, Tom, William, Mary, Janetta, James, Henry
                                                        married_____
(John McEwen was born 12-18-1851, died in 1940. Both he and his   James, Mary Etta, Lucinda
father, George Rex, homesteaded in Republic County, Kansas. Some   (b.10-1-1859;
records show adjacent quarters, four miles east of Republic.)   d. 1940)

Lewis Elmer McEwen, Bertha May, Sylvia O'Resla, Lawrence Le Roy
(b.3-7-1883;   (b.3-2-1887; (b. 3-22-1894; (b. 5-3-1896;
d.8-1-1952)   d.6-17-1968) d.12-29-1894) d. 5-23-1961)   Ethel Nina Harsh
                            married_____   (b. 2-17-1885;
                                                                     (d. 5-10-1960)
                Velma I., Gerald Earl McEwen, Leonard Russell
                (b.2-4-1906; (b.4-30-1907;   b.2-3-1911;
                d.8-26-1906) d.7-9-1944)   d.2-??-1966)

                        John Rufus Pennington--married--Elizabeth Mary ??????

                                                        William Wiley Stewart--married--Ida Eleanor Kelly

                                        Charles Arthur Pennington--married--Hazel Pearl Stewart
                                        (b. 9-30-1885; d.Mar. 1936)   (b.3-24-1889;
                                                                            d.4-26-1931)

                                Percy, Charles Stewart, Marie Laverne Pennington, Maurice Hubert
                                                (b.8-12-1913; d.1-1-1991)
                                married_____
                                (Place of marriage:
                                Clay Center, Clay County,
                                Nebraska. October 2, 1931)
                                                                                    married_____ Wilbur G. Plautz
                                                                                                    (b.3-18-1917;
                                                                                                     d.8-4-1989)
                                                                                    (Place of marriage:
                                                                                    York, York County,
                                                                                    Nebraska. February 20, 1948)

                Beverly Jean, Larry Burdette McEwen, Geraldine Marie, Sandra Elaine, Deborah Marie Plautz
                (b/d 6-5-1932)   (b. 8-4-1934)   (b. 5-10-1936)   (b.12-16-1944) (b. 9-26-1949)

                                                                                Rudolph Carlson--married--Gladys Walgreen

                                                                        Carl Rudolph, Mary, JoAnne Loraine Carlson
                                                                                            (b. 10-3-1934)
Charlotte Evelyn Alloway
(b. 12-16-1945)_____married_____   married_____
                                                                    (Place of marriage: Osceola, Polk County, Nebraska, February 3, 1956)
        (Place of marriage: Las Vegas, Clark County,   (Divorced May, 1975, Carlinville, Macoupin County, Illinois)
        Nevada, February 14, 1978)
                                                                                        Russell Lacy--married--Karen Stark

                        Diana Jo McEwen   Sheila Jo McEwen
                        (b. 11-28-1957)   (b. 5-6-1967)   Rodney D. Lacy
Louis Stiles   (b. 8-20-1966)
(b. 10-??-56)_____married_____   married____

(Handwritten record found at George McEwen residence)

"George Rex McEwen was born in Glasgow, Scotland on June 2nd, 1823.
First came to U.S.A. looking for a younger brother and stopped in ~~Andrew~~
Chicago and Wisconsin, returning to Scotland for a few years. The
second time came to Canada, settled at Carlton, Lenrick Co., Ontario ~~Wester~~
and married there to Sarah Elizabeth Brindel, daughter of Lord John (No)
Brindel of the house of Parliment of Nara, Tipperary Co., Ireland,
from his first marriage to Miss McMahan, and after his first wife's (Isabelle)
death — he married again, but do not know her name. [died in western Canada]

Isabelle

BRINDEL McMahan — d'in Canada — 1 child — Isabeel — ~~2nd~~
George and Sarah E. Brindel — b. 1849/30 — being ? Ireland

daughter
b A? – 18 4 ?

1. Isabella married 1) Ed Cronan, son Edwin
               2) George Comer, daughter Ida, son George
               3) Andrew Minard

daughter
P Sarah
Canada

2. Sarah Elizabeth married John Edward Parker, son John, Jr. — Parker

3. John born 12-18-1851 married Mary Etta Rowley — born in Canada a — 1st child
   infant son died at birth
   Louis Elmer born March 7, 1883
   Elmer Bertha May born March 2, 1887
   Sylvia O'Resla born March 22, 1894 — died
   Lawrence LeRoy born May 2, 1896 — 1 son

4. Margaret married Jessie Beers, son Issac Beers

5. George, single, cigar maker — younger

Younger

6. Agnes married Alexander Cole, daughter Udona married John McNutt
   Later Agnes married Williams

Thomas

7. Tom married Millie Quick — (MATAUDEN-QUICK) — ?
   Delbert — Md-Helen Marie Seeley — Thompson's
   Sylvia — Md — a de — Bith — ? age
   Gistina — Robert — Killed & Raped — OK
   Edithe — ~~killed OK~~ ?
   Max

8. William married Lena Titus June 28th — 1886 — Married
   Pery   1. Ray   2. Maude ? — when she died of ?
   Nora — Ogden Hawley
   Lee McEwen + Gladys (Okley) McEwen
   Stella — Md-IRA, Seeley — sister-Helen M. Seeley-Md-Stella-Cous A-Delbert
   Elsie
   Teddy

b-1866 ~9. Mary

b-1868 10. Janetta married brother of George Marsh, has 27 children, I can't remember their names

1870 12-kids 11. James married Bell Bliss, son Alvia, then married Della
left his family & never come └Clarence *Lydia lives in Bernongnore MS*
wa back
                    LeRoy
                    Floyd
                    Clifford
                    Claude
                    Alta
                    Stella
                    Jeanettie
                    Robert
                    Beulah
                    Maxine

b-1872-? 12. Henry don't know anything about him - George McEwen Son
we in KS

Louis Elmer McEwen was born 4 miles east of Republic, Kansas March 7, 1883
Bertha May McEwen was born 4 miles east of Republic, Kansas March 2, 1887
Laurence LeRoy McEwen was born 4 miles east of Republic, Kansas May 30, 1890
Sylvia Oresta was born 4 miles east of Republic, Kansas March 22, 1894,
    died December 29, 1894"

Lawrence LeRoy - side Stiffin - Republic KS)
Son - Daniel McEwen d-2005

#2

George Rex And Sarah E. Brindel McEwen
7 Chid
Tom - Married Millie Matalack
Millie was married beFor to a [Quick] - a son
Quick. was in the Cow, Boy. Hall oF Fame in OKla.
Tom and Millie
5 children

1 Delbert McEwen married the sister oF Ira Seeley.
who is Helen Seeley - the sister in law oF Stella McEwe
2 Sylva -   daughter is Bill. who lives in OKla.City, OK
(3) Jessie. 4. Christina, 5. Max

George Rex McEwen -- 9th child of 1st Gen Lord and Lady Brindle of Ireland – may of been in Scotland. Daughter Brindle Md 2nd Gen John McEwen Sir – b. abt 1780 – Scotland – 8th gen – 8 – son's – 1st – John McEwen Jr. & Agnes – both born the same year – two daughters – George Rex McEwen Md – Isabelle McMahon – daughter Isabelle McEwen – Md - 3 times. George Md -2nd ? – 3rd are Great Grand Mother – Sarah Elizabeth Brindle – She Md 1st John Brindle & was to have a baby – He died 2nd on Family Sheet – Sarah Elizabeth Brindle Parker

Are Great Grand Mother Sarah – lived with one of her daughters.

Photos & Family

Zoe 1st Grade (Blond hair, Far right, Back Row)

Darlene & John McEwen
July 17, 1938

Marvin ~ Zoe McEwen

Diana & Leila

Tim & wife Cheryl
Jenny (Adopted Daughter)
& friend

Zoe & Siblings

Paul & Zoe & Kids

Paul & Zoe Golden & Kids (+ ex-Daughter-In-Law)

Paul & Zoe Golden

Dan Golden & Family

Paul Golden

Paul Golden

Zoe Golden
22 or 23 Years Old, Portland, Oregon

Leota's Family

Leota Allen

Zoe's Mom & Kenny

Leota M. McEwen-Baker-Saylor-Allen

Leota M. McEwen-Baker-Saylor-Allen of Pacific died in Federal Way Feb. 9, 1996. She was 76.

She was born in Lamar, Colo., on Jan. 21, 1920. She had lived in the Valley area 30 years.

She worked as a tool clerk for the aerospace industry. She was a member of the Auburn Elks PM, the Ladies of the Moose and a charter member of Toledo Oregon Trail Post No. 3429 Auxiliary of the Veterans of Foreign Wars.

She is survived by two sons, LeRoy Baker of Libby, Mont., and Harry Wayne Baker of Kent; three daughters, W. Darlene Chambliss of Pacific, Shirley McKenzie of Columbia Falls, Mont., and Joyce Thackeray of Yakima; four brothers, Kenneth and John McEwen, both of Toledo, and Melvin and Marvin McEwen, both of Yakima; three sisters, Gladys Bowen of Kila, Mont., Elzora Golden of Auburn, and Trula Wassik of California; his mother, Gladys McEwen of Toledo; a stepdaughter, Myrtle McLennan of Grants Pass, Ore.; a stepson, Clyde Baker of Bellingham; 14 grandchildren; 19 great-grandchildren; and two great-great-grandchildren.

A funeral service is 10 a.m. today at Price-Helton Funeral Chapel in Auburn. She will be buried at Sticklin Cemetery in Centralia. Arrangements by Price-Helton Funeral Chapel.

Ron & Gloria
helped Pastors
Dave & Alice
Darroch with First
Girl's Home

Bev Wheeler &
Daughter

Missionaries that
Paul & Zoe supported

Drylands, Colorado

Lee McEwen, 1917 in the
Army Ft. Leavenworth, KS

Zoe's Dad's side (All boys)

William & Lannie McEwen
Grandpa & Grandma

Dad in Army

Zoe's Mom in the Drylands

Mom's Father & Family

Zoe's Dad (1919)

Zoe's Grandma

Zoe's Relatives

Darlene
Zoe's Niece

Jamie's Mother.(Lady on left side, back row) Saw Her Four Kids She Lost Right Before She Died

Zoe McEwen, age 14

Zoe McEwen, 15-years-old

Lana ~ Two Boys

Lana & Friend (right)

Zoe, Mother, Kenny & Trula

Bennetts: Bill & wife Judy
(Zoe lived with them)

I Remember When...

I Remember When...

A story from Lelia...Zoe & Paul's oldest daughter

When I was younger, we were going to go on a small trip somewhere. My mom began to pace. I asked when we were going to leave and she said she was burdened and she continued to pray.

I knew what that meant and so I didn't say anything more. She later said, it's okay to go now.

We were traveling in the car for a little while and came to an area of the freeway that looked mostly deserted. There were officers in the middle of the freeway.

My mom slowed down and rolled her window down. She said, "Officer, what is going on?"

The officer said that there was a man on the freeway shooting at cars. She said, "About how long ago was that?"

He told her and we drove on. Had we left at the original time, we might have been one of those cars.

Mom said she shared this with people at her class reunion. She wanted to make sure they all knew Jesus. We were in a phone store and Mom shared with a man that was waiting to be called. There was another man with a small boy next to him. The little boy was looking at an electronic device.

The dad was probably trying to keep him quiet. After my mom shared with the man, he was called to one of the desks. The other man with the little boy turned to her and said he had heard what she had shared with the man and was very excited about it.

The man went to a church in the area and said he was originally from Africa. My mom has shared Jesus with many people. She told me that she shared with lots of people when we lived in Oakland, California. They became believers.

She also shared with the Purfoys who we had known for years. They had become involved with the Jim Jones group. She told them they needed to get away from that church. They got out of that group just in time. We found out that many people involved with that group died in Guyana.

Author's Note

Thank you to Pastor Dave and Alice Darroch for being so faithful for so many years. I am grateful. We love Spokane Dream Center and our church family there so much.

Thanks to Barbara Tevis, who has been such a good friend.

Thanks to Tom Hamilton, Sr. and Tom Hamilton, Jr. and their whole family has been such a blessing to me.

A special thanks to Barb Hollace for all your efforts on this book. You have been a true friend, true prayer warrior. Love the things God does through us.

Thanks to Ben Matheson, chiropractor in Kennewick has been a blessing to me and also his mother, Cindy.

Thanks to D'Arcy Dormaier and family, they have been a great inspiration to us through God's Word.

Thanks to George and Margaret Lopez who have been such a blessing through my illness. Love you, kids.

Thanks to my granddaughter and her husband, Amber and Jason Alderman for taking such good care of us and inviting us into your home. You have been such a blessing.

Thanks to our children and their families. Our beloved daughters, Diana and Lelia and all they have done for us. Also our two sons, Tim and Dan, and the blessings they have been to us.

And what a blessing my grandchildren and great-grandchildren have been in our lives. Thank you!

And so many others, you know who you are. God bless you!

168

Favorite Bible Verses

Zoe's most favorite Bible verse

John 3:16 NJKV
For God so loved the world that He gave His only begotten Son,
that whoever believes in Him should not perish but have everlasting life.

Favorite Bible Verse to lead souls to Christ

Romans 10:9-10 NKJV
That if you confess with your mouth the Lord Jesus and believe in your heart that God has raised Him from the dead, you will be saved. For with the heart one believes unto righteousness, and with the mouth confession is made unto salvation.

Bible Verse Zoe has held on to during her healing journey

Psalm 23:1 NKJV
The Lord is my shepherd;
I shall not want.

www.ingramcontent.com/pod-product-compliance
Lightning Source LLC
LaVergne TN
LVHW061332060426
835512LV00017B/2667